LOOK
BACK,
LEAP
FORWARD

OTHER BOOKS BY GARY L. MCINTOSH

The Exodus Principle
Three Generations
Make Room for the Boom . . . or Bust
One Size Doesn't Fit All
Staff Your Church for Growth

With Samuel D. Rima Sr.
Overcoming the Dark Side of Leadership

With Glen S. Martin
Creating Community
Finding Them, Keeping Them
The Issachar Factor

With Robert Edmondson
It Only Hurts on Monday

LOOK BACK, LEAP FORWARD

BUILDING YOUR CHURCH ON THE VALUES OF THE PAST

GARY L. McINTOSH

Baker Books

A Division of Baker Book House Co
Grand Rapids, Michigan 49516

© 2001 by Gary L. McIntosh

Published by Baker Books
a division of Baker Book House Company
P.O. Box 6287, Grand Rapids, MI 49516-6287

Printed in the United States of America

Library of Congress Cataloging-in-Publication Data

McIntosh, Gary, 1947–
    Look back, leap forward : building your church on the values of the
past / Gary L. McIntosh.
        p.   cm.
    ISBN 0-8010-9112-8
    1. Church growth. I. Title.

BV652.25 .M3185 2001
254'.5—dc21   2001035723

Most Scripture quotations are taken from the NEW AMERICAN STAN-DARD BIBLE ®. Copyright © The Lockman Foundation 1960, 1962, 1963, 1968, 1971, 1972, 1973, 1975, 1977, 1995. Used by permission.

Other translations quoted are the New King James Version (pp. 20–21), The Living Bible (p. 21), the New International Version (p. 114).

For current information about all releases from Baker Book House, visit our web site:
                    http://www.bakerbooks.com

CONTENTS

INTRODUCTION

SOMEONE ONCE REMARKED that the only constant in life is change. While all of us appreciate many of the changes taking place—especially those that bring comfort to our lives—many dislike the apparent loss of beloved programs and values in our churches. Like an anonymous person once remarked, "I like progress; it is change I cannot stand." If you are someone who is frustrated with the changes going on around and in your church, *Look Back, Leap Forward* will provide insights on how to build the future of your church on the values of its past.

It is the story of one person who learned that *when you are not sure where you are going, you need to look to where you have been.* My purpose in telling Wendy's story is to pass along to you what she learned in the hope that it will help you build a better future for your church.

The story is actually a compilation of the experiences of several different churches and how they established new vision for the future by building on traditional, biblical values. Any similarities between the characters and examples in the story and those of any person or church are purely coincidental.

1

THE BEST FUTURE

I T WAS ONE OF THOSE DAYS when I just could not keep my mind on the road. As I turned into the church parking lot, it suddenly dawned on me that I had driven the last few blocks in a daze. The truth is I did not even remember driving the last few blocks! I guess my subconscious mind kept me moving along safely. Or perhaps it was my guardian angel.

I had been mentally scolding myself for accepting the position of chairperson of my church's vision planning team. What was I thinking? Who was I to assume I could lead this team to develop a plan to renew our church's direction? What insights could I bring to the discussion that would be helpful? Why had I agreed to it?

Yes, my thoughts had distracted me and I was unable to concentrate on my driving. As I looked at it, my qualifications seemed pretty slim: first grade teacher for five years, loving wife, and mother of three children. From my point of view, these were not strong qualifications for leading the team assigned to design a new vision and plan for the future of my church.

That is why I had asked for an appointment with my pastor. I was sure he had made a mistake in asking me to be the team leader. I would remind him of my limited experience and qualifications, and I was sure he would agree to let me step down from this leadership position.

Mary, the pastor's secretary, greeted me as I entered the office complex of my church. We chatted for a couple of minutes and then she motioned to Pastor Steve's open door. "Go right in, Wendy."

As I entered Pastor Steve's office, I was surprised by the nervousness I felt. We had been friends for years and I usually found him easy to talk with. Never before, though, had I turned down a job he asked me to do. We didn't get right into that, though. We spent nearly half an hour talking about our families. This is one of the things I like about my pastor. He always seems to be concerned about my family.

Finally I said, "Pastor." I cleared my throat and went on, "I really think I agreed too quickly to accept the position of chairperson for our vision planning team."

"Oh! Why is that?" Pastor Steve asked frowning.

"Well, I have been thinking about this a lot lately and I really don't think I am qualified for the job."

"I see," Steve mumbled. "Tell me more."

"I just do not see what I have to offer the vision planning team or the church," I blurted. "I don't have any great ideas about how to turn our church around, and my experience is pretty much with young children. Also, I don't have the answers to our church's current plateauing concern. I realize we need some new direction, but I'm not sure I'm the one to provide the answers."

"Yes, I can see how you might feel unqualified," Steve nodded. "But I didn't ask you to be the team leader because you have all the answers."

"Really?" I asked, a bit surprised. "Then why did you ask me to be the chairperson?"

"Frankly," Steve continued, "I was looking for someone who could lead a team. Do you remember the last couple of years how you led the children's department to set new goals?"

"Yes, but the children's department is made up of children," I gently reminded him.

"That's true," Pastor Steve agreed, "but the team you worked with were adult leaders, not children, and you did an outstanding job of leading them. I am certain you are the right person to lead our planning team. You have the ability to build unity, and that's what we need. Besides," Pastor Steve continued, "I want someone to lead this team who has no axe to grind."

"No axe to grind?" I echoed.

"Yes, no axe to grind. I am convinced our church is in need of a new vision. Many people in our church will admit that. However, some think we need to go back to doing ministry the way we used to thirty, forty, or even fifty years ago. They think we have abandoned our traditional values, and we need to restore old programs to remain faithful to the Bible. Then others in our church are demanding that we abandon our past and use new forms of ministry that are working better in other churches today. Some want us to change our name and even target our Sunday services totally to the unchurched in our community."

"I have heard people talking about these ideas myself," I said, confirming Pastor Steve's observations.

"The debate over whether we revive old ministries or adopt new ones could be dangerous," Pastor Steve confessed. "I read once that Winston Churchill said: 'If we open a quarrel between the past and the present, we shall find we have lost the future.' Wendy, I'm a little afraid that if we don't develop a new vision for the future of our church, we may find our church in a major quarrel that will destroy our future. One of the reasons I asked you to lead our vision planning team is that you seem to appreciate our church's past while looking forward to our future."

"Okay, Pastor Steve, I can see your point. It's important that our church come to an agreement on the future. It's also true that I see value in our past as well as hope for our future as a church but I still fail to see how I can help."

> IF WE OPEN A QUARREL BETWEEN THE PAST AND THE PRESENT, WE SHALL FIND WE HAVE LOST THE FUTURE.

"What I'm saying," Pastor Steve raised his voice as he stood up from his desk, "is I need a team leader who can help us look back and leap forward."

I hesitated, trying to grasp what he had said. "I'm not sure what you mean by 'look back and leap forward,'" I admitted.

"Let me explain it this way," Pastor Steve said. "I like to read historical novels about other countries in the world. Once I was reading a novel about Australia and discovered an interesting fact. When Australia was a new nation, its leaders designed a crest to represent their newly formed country. Two animals—

> LOOK BACK AND LEAP FORWARD!

the kangaroo and the emu—stood on each side of the crest. These two particular animals were chosen because of a unique common characteristic. While kangaroos and emus can turn their heads to glance backward to get their bearings, they always move forward. Though each animal is very swift afoot, often reaching speeds of thirty miles per hour, neither is able to walk backwards. In other words, kangaroos and emus look back but leap forward."

13

> **WE LIVE LIFE FORWARD BY UNDERSTANDING IT BACKWARD.**

"What you're saying," I summarized, "is that it's okay for our church to look back, as long as it points us to the future. Is that correct?"

"Yes, I think you have the basic idea," Pastor Steve assured me. "I was introduced to this concept last year by Bob Morrison, a pastor friend of mine. He likes to say, 'We live life forward by understanding it backward.' In fact, if you are willing to be the chairperson of our vision planning team, I'd like for you to visit him and meet with members of his team. I think they'll be able to give you some good pointers on how to lead such a team."

"You know, Pastor Steve, I'm honestly interested in helping our church become healthy and faithful in ministry. I guess it wouldn't hurt for me to meet with Pastor Morrison to gain some additional perspective on the planning process. However, I'd like to keep the final decision on whether I'll accept the chairperson position open until after I've had a chance to think it through a little longer."

"Fine. Fine!" Pastor Steve replied with obvious delight that I was willing to give the idea further consideration.

"So what's our next step?" I asked as I stood to leave.

"Why don't I set up a meeting between you and Pastor Morrison for next week. Would Tuesday morning work for you?"

"As long as it's after 9:00 so I can drop my youngest off at kindergarten," I said.

"Good. I'll take care of it and call you tomorrow to confirm the time."

"Sounds fine," I said as I walked toward the door.

"One more thing, Wendy," Pastor Steve stopped me just as I was leaving. "Here is a copy of a cartoon I found that illustrates what we've been discussing. Why don't you take it with you and read it when you have the chance."

"Will do," I said as I put the cartoon in my purse. "Talk with you tomorrow."

I forgot about the cartoon until later that evening after I had put my children to bed. My husband and I finally found time to sit down together over a cup of hot tea and discuss my conversation with the pastor earlier that day when I remembered the cartoon and took it out to read. In the cartoon Calvin and

> **LOOK BOTH WAYS DOWN THE ROAD.**

Hobbes are walking down the street, and Calvin says, "You could step in the road tomorrow and—wham—you get hit by a cement truck. That's why my motto is *Live for today*. What's your motto, Hobbes?" Hobbes answers, "Look both ways down the road."

2

LOOK BOTH WAYS

I T WAS VERY CHARACTERISTIC of Pastor Steve to use a cartoon to get me thinking. He is fond of using cartoons in his Sunday sermons, so I was not surprised he gave me one about Calvin and Hobbes as I left his office last week.

I was thinking about the need to look both ways—to the past and the future—when developing a new direction for my church. I was anxious to meet Bob Morrison and find out how the vision planning team functions at his church.

As he promised, Pastor Steve set up a meeting with Bob Morrison for me. "Thanks for taking time to meet with me today," I said as I entered Bob's office.

"I understand you are interested in learning how to look back and leap forward," Bob grinned at me.

"I can see Pastor Steve filled you in on our conversation," I replied.

"Yes, he did."

"Well, what does it mean to you when you say we must look back and leap forward?" I asked.

"That's a good place to begin. Essentially I have discovered that one cannot have a real vision for the future without a sense of history."

"Expand on that a little," I requested.

> **ONE CANNOT HAVE A REAL VISION FOR THE FUTURE WITHOUT A SENSE OF HISTORY.**

"I think the past is a record of the values that should propel us into the future," Bob continued. "As we move toward the future, it is important that we look back to discover the values that give meaning to our ministries and then leap forward by building on our values to take hold of new opportunities. Unfortunately the strong pull toward the future may cause us to overlook the past."

"I think I know what you mean," I said. "There are quite a number of people in my church who believe we've forgotten the past. We never seem to sing the old hymns anymore, listen to stories from the past, or consider the way ministry used to be done."

"Yes, that is often true, but we have to be careful," Bob cautioned. "If looking back promotes a *Band-*

Aid mentality of survival in an effort to hold the church together by looking to the good old days for affirmation, then looking back is not good. I've discovered that when a church looks to the past for its sense of pride, it leads to dwelling too much on past successes. Yet when a church looks to the past to discover its values, it can be a powerful link to the future. I'm really not one to dwell in the past too much. I think that we should only look back so that we can leap ahead. As I usually say, the past is for remembering not reliving."

> **THE PAST IS FOR REMEMBERING NOT RELIVING.**

"I see what you mean," I said as I wrote down some thoughts to ponder later. Over the years, I have developed the habit of writing things down in a notebook. One thing to my credit: I am well organized. My notes included the following:

Insights for looking back, leaping forward

- *We live life forward by understanding it backward.*
- *It's important to look both ways down the road.*
- *The past is for remembering not reliving.*

"However," Bob spoke as I wrote, "looking back is necessary to fund a powerful future. Martin Marty, a church historian at the University of Chicago, calls this 'finding a usable future in our past.'"

"This all makes sense," I interrupted, "but is it biblical to look back? In my Tuesday morning Bible class we've been studying Philippians. In that book the apostle Paul says that he forgets what is behind him and looks forward to the future."

"Yes, that's correct," Bob affirmed. "That's Philippians chapter three, verse thirteen. However, Paul is talking about his desire to become like Christ. He means that he doesn't want to put his confidence in fleshly concerns that once were important to him, like his ethnic heritage and training. In short, he is looking only to his faith in becoming more like Christ.

"There are other biblical passages, however, that point out the importance of remembering the past," Bob added. "Joshua might have said, A good past is the best future. You remember the story in Joshua chapter four, verses one through twenty-four. After all the people of Israel had finished crossing the Jordan River, the Lord spoke to Joshua and commanded that twelve stones be removed from the river and set up as a memorial. After the stones were set up in Gilgal, Joshua explained the reason. Let me read it to you.

> A GOOD PAST IS
> THE BEST FUTURE.

When your children ask their fathers in time to come, saying, "What are these stones?" then you shall let your children know, saying, "Israel crossed the Jordan on dry land"; for the LORD your God dried up the waters of the Jordan before you until you had

crossed over, as the LORD your God did to the Red
Sea, which He dried up before us until we had
crossed over, that all the peoples of the earth may
know the hand of the LORD, that it is mighty, that
you may fear the LORD your God forever.

"The Lord knew that understanding the values
of the past is crucial for designing a new future.
Thus he commanded that whenever the nation of
Israel struggled with determining direction, the
people should always look to the past to rediscover
their core values."

"I never thought of that passage in that way
before," I said.

"Another passage that says it differently is Psalm
twenty-two, verses thirty and thirty-one. The Living Bible paraphrases it in this way. 'Our children
too shall serve him, for they shall hear from us
about the wonders of the Lord; generations yet
unborn shall hear of all the miracles he did for us.'"

"There is a great deal of talk today about defining a church's core values," I said. "Is it possible to
define our values without looking at the past?"

"It is a mistake to think that we create our values in a vacuum. The truth is we discover them by
looking to the past," Bob explained. "Just as the
people of Israel looked to the past to rebuild their
values, we must look back to our church's past to
reconstruct ours. We need to create sort of a conversation with the past. I like how Kiyoko Takeda,
a professor at International Christian University in

Tokyo, says it: 'Recognizing what we have done in the past is recognition of ourselves. By conducting a dialogue with our past, we are searching how to go forward.' Remember: When you aren't sure where you are going, look to where you've been."

"So, how far back should we look?" I quizzed.

"I'd say it's good to look as far back as possible. I don't know where I heard this, but it's reported that Winston Churchill once said, 'The farther backward you can look, the farther forward you can see.' That makes sense to me."

> **WHEN YOU AREN'T SURE WHERE YOU ARE GOING, LOOK TO WHERE YOU'VE BEEN.**

"Okay, I can see that it is biblical to look both ways—backward and forward. So what comes next?"

"I think the next step is to talk about the life cycle of a church," Bob replied. "Do you have a little more time?"

"Yes, I need to pick up my son at 11:45, but I can spend a little more time talking about looking back and leaping forward," I laughed.

"Good." Bob seemed pleased that I could stay a little longer. "Let's go into the conference room so I can use the whiteboard." He stood and walked toward the door.

"Would you like something to drink?" he asked. "We have several kinds of soda."

"Yes, that sounds good."

After picking up a soda in the church's kitchen, Bob and I headed to the conference room so he could use the whiteboard. While he looked for pens for writing on the board, I took a moment to add some thoughts to my notebook.

Insights for looking back, leaping forward

- *We live life forward by understanding it backward.*
- *It's important to look both ways down the road.*
- *The past is for remembering not reliving.*
- *A good past is the best future. Key Scripture: Joshua 4.*
- *When you're not sure where you're going, look to where you've been.*

3

ST. JOHN'S SYNDROME
The Plateauing Church

WHAT DID YOU MEAN that it would be good for me to understand the life cycle of a church?" I asked as I finished writing in my notebook.

"Well, let me begin by sketching a life cycle with which you are familiar."

Bob drew the following on his whiteboard.

"As you know, we all live through a predictable life cycle that begins with birth, continues through adulthood, and ends in death," Bob said.

"Yes, this is normal for most of us," I spoke as I sketched the life cycle in my notebook.

"What most people in our churches don't realize," Bob continued, "is that there is also a normal

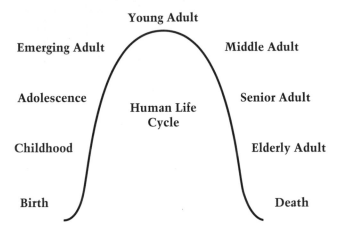

life cycle for churches. Here, let me show you by changing the words on my first drawing."

Bob then made a few changes on his first chart and created the following.

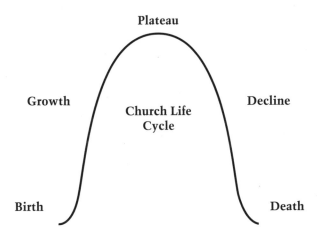

"Most churches go through this cycle of birth and growth, followed by a period of plateau, and then eventual decline and death," Bob explained.

"My husband and I were involved in the birth of a new church right after we were married," I mentioned. "We remember it as a time of real excitement, sort of like when we had our first child."

"That's a good analogy," Bob said. "Back when my wife and I had our first child, I was able to go into the delivery room with her. Immediately after our daughter was born, the nurse placed her in my arms. As I looked into her brown eyes, I had such hope for her future. I remember feeling that she might grow up to be a teacher like her grandmother."

"My husband had a similar experience," I said.

"When the birth of a church takes place, there is often a very similar feeling of excitement and hope for the future. This vision propels the church to experience growth over the next three to five years. In fact this early vision of the future may even carry a church for ten to twenty years or more, depending on the expanse of the vision. It's sort of like tracking your children through childhood, adolescence, on into college. It's great to see them developing along the way."

"That's something I'm looking forward to," I said, "but our children are still in the childhood stage."

"My advice is enjoy every minute of it," Bob encouraged. "The time goes fast. Thinking of the church life cycle again," he returned to the point of our conversation, "eventually a church moves onto a plateau, which may last from twenty to sixty years. A lot of good ministry takes place during this time of plateau. Missionaries are sent to the field, people are won to Christ, children are discipled, but ever so slowly the church experiences more plateauing than growth. Actually a better way to draw the typical life cycle of a church is like this." Bob changed his drawing to look like the following.

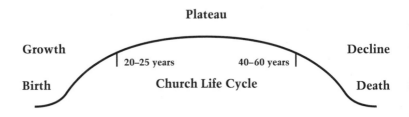

"This drawing actually pictures what takes place in a church. The growth phase of a church normally lasts about twenty to twenty-five years. While there are always exceptions, for most churches the best years of growth are over by the church's twenty-fifth birthday. It's not that the remaining years are bad ones," Bob quickly added, "but there is a slowing of growth as the church moves into a maintenance mode of ministry. Unfortunately," Bob added, "if this plateauing is left unchallenged, the eventual result is decline and often death of the church."

"What do you mean by 'death of the church'? I don't like to think about churches dying," I explained.

"A church dies when it closes its doors or when it becomes so ineffective that it no longer carries out the Great Commission," Bob said. "No one really knows for sure, but the best estimates are that about four thousand churches actually close their doors every year. There are many others that remain open but are not fulfilling their purpose. There's a cute story that illustrates this well. It seems that a young boy went fishing with his grandfather. As they walked from their car to the lake, they happened on a small turtle. Immediately the grandfather took out his pocket knife and cut off the turtle's head to use as bait. After fishing for a short while, the boy and his grandfather walked back to their car to eat their picnic lunch. When they walked by the turtle's body, the boy noticed it was moving. He exclaimed, 'Grandpa! That turtle's still alive!'

"His grandfather replied, 'No, he's dead. He just doesn't know it yet.'

"You see, many churches are like that turtle—so ineffective they are dead. They just don't realize it yet."

"Can this be changed?" I quizzed.

"Yes, it can," Bob assured me, "but this life cycle is so predictable it has been named St. John's Syndrome."

"That's a strange name," I said. "How did it come to be called that?"

"The name comes from the last book of the Bible, Revelation. As you may recall, St. John received a vision while he was exiled on the Island of Patmos. In the first part of his vision, he saw what has come to be called the Seven Churches of Revelation."

"Our pastor preached on that passage last year," I said. "As I remember it, the churches had all started out well but gradually became less effective as they grew older."

"Exactly!" Bob seemed pleased that I had grasped the key aspect of the story. "St. John's Syndrome is the tendency of churches to become less effective the longer they are in existence."

"Okay," I pointed out, "I get the concept. So, is a church doomed to follow this life cycle?"

"No, it's not!" Bob stated rather firmly. "I call this the life cycle of a church *without* intervention. Churches don't have to blindly travel this path. They can take action to restore the vitality they once experienced."

"So how does such a renewal take place?" I prodded.

"By looking back and leaping forward," Bob grinned.

"Okay, I'm game. What's the key?" I asked.

"Think back with me to my story of holding my daughter right after she had been born. My thoughts were full of dreams for my daughter. She might become a teacher, perhaps the executive of a large company, or maybe a governor. Now that she is twenty-one, I know that one of those dreams has been realized. She is a teacher. Other goals will likely never come true. She's not headed toward being a governor."

"Sounds like a natural course of events to me."

"You're right," Bob agreed. "There is also a natural course of events for a church. The reason churches plateau after twenty to twenty-five years is that they have fulfilled their original vision. Most churches begin with a clear sense of their values around which they build a vision for the future. It takes only about ten to twenty-five years to fulfill most of their dreams. Unfortunately the majority of churches never develop a new dream or vision for the future. In fact I've heard it said that the saddest day in the life of a church is when they burn the church's mortgage."

"Why is that?" I was surprised. "I'd think that finally paying off the church's mortgage would be a great day."

"In a way it is," Bob agreed. "Unfortunately, though, most churches never replace the dream of paying off the church's mortgage with a new vision for the future. Thus the church begins to plateau, which leads to an eventual decline."

"So, the key to overcoming St. John's Syndrome is to rediscover a church's values and then develop a new dream for the future based on those values. Is that correct?"

"Exactly," Bob affirmed. "Let me add something to my last drawing. The life cycle of a church with a new dream would look like this."

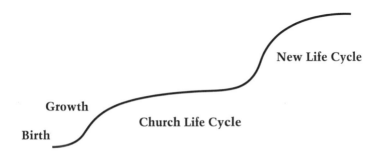

"Whenever a church finds itself searching for a new direction, it must look back to rediscover its essential values, and then leap forward by developing a new dream for the future based on those values. For long-term growth, a church must start a new life cycle by looking back and leaping forward about every ten years."

"This all makes good sense, but how does one guide a church to look back and leap forward?" I asked.

"I'd like to answer that, but I need to leave to get to another meeting. Besides, I want to avoid the Goethe Syndrome," Bob explained.

"The Goethe Syndrome? What's that?"

"Goethe, the great eighteenth-century German poet, supposedly knew everything that was to be known in his age. Of course, he really didn't know everything, and neither do I. So, while I'd enjoy trying to give you all the answers, I think it would be best if you met with some of the members of our vision planning team. They can explain the practical steps of how to look back and leap forward better than I can."

"Sounds like a good idea."

"Let's go talk to my secretary," Bob suggested. "She will give you a list of our vision planning team members, and you can contact them to set up individual meetings. I'd suggest you meet with Marvin Woods first."

Pastor Bob's secretary printed out Marvin Woods's address and phone number from her computer for me before I left the office. Later that evening I called Marvin and set up an appointment. Marvin is the chairperson of Pastor Bob's vision planning team. We decided to spend a day talking about developing vision and related topics.

After my talk with Pastor Bob, this is what I had in my notebook:

Insights for looking back, leaping forward

- We live life forward by understanding it backward.
- It's important to look both ways down the road.
- The past is for remembering not reliving.
- A good past is the best future. Key Scripture: Joshua 4.
- When you're not sure where you're going, look to where you've been.
- St. John's Syndrome: the tendency of a church to become less effective as it ages. Key Scripture: Revelation 2-3.

4

TEAM TOGETHER
For the Present and the Future

THE MOMENT I WALKED into Marvin Woods's office, I knew he was just the person to help me delve deeper into the process of helping my church look back and leap forward. On his desk is this plaque:

Together
Everyone
Accomplishes
More

As I sat down, I said, "I noticed your plaque on teams. How important is teamwork in helping a church look back and leap forward?"

Laughing, Mr. Woods said, "I can see you've met with our senior pastor. He's always talking about the importance of looking back and leaping forward. To answer your question, we find that teamwork is crucial to looking back and leaping forward. In fact we actually divide our vision planning team into two subteams."

"I'll bet one team looks back and the other looks forward. Am I right?"

"Yes and no. Actually both teams look back. The difference is one team looks back to get ideas on how to improve the present, while the other team looks back to get ideas on how to create the future. The first team says, 'Together, we improve the present.' The second team says, 'Together, we create the future.'"

"Tell me more, Mr. Woods," I said as I added his comments to my notebook.

"Please call me Marvin," he began. "There's no need for formality.

"We discovered by trial and error that some people are passionate about improving the present church ministry. I think the term that is being used today is 'continuous improvement.' If you ask these people to dream about the future of the church, they just can't seem to do it. They see the present picture very well but have a hard time thinking long-term for the future. So instead of trying to force them to envision the future of our church's ministry, we let them focus on what they find easy to do—improve the present. On the other hand, some of our people like to dream about what our church can become in the next few years. They really enjoy projecting ideas into the future. If we were to ask them to work on improving the present, they would be bored. So we have them focus on how to build the future of our church."

"It seems like a simple idea," I commented. "Why don't more churches do this?"

> **IT'S HARD TO MAKE PLANS TO DRAIN THE SWAMP WHEN THE ALLIGATORS ARE BITING.**

"Part of the reason is that the pressures of the present situation are so demanding it causes churches to invest great energy in preserving what they are already doing, rather than designing the future. The old proverb is true: It's hard to make plans to drain the swamp when the alligators are biting."

I laughed. "It's still a sound idea. How did you come up with this plan?"

"We borrowed the idea from Dr. Ken Blanchard, a popular speaker on developing vision. He suggests dividing into two teams that he calls a 'P team' and an 'F team.' As you might suspect, the P stands for present, and the F stands for future. The way we've divided up the focus is the P team looks back to our church's core values to see if we can improve our current ministries. The F team looks back to our core values to create the future."

"So how do you decide who fits on which team?"

"We ask them to answer these questions," Marvin answered, as he began reading from a paper on his desk.

1. Would you rather dream about the future or fix the present?
2. Would you rather design a new program or improve an existing one?
3. Would you rather do the right things or do things right?
4. Would you rather be innovative or effective?
5. Would you rather develop ministry for future members or develop ministry for members who are already here?

As you might guess, the first part of each question is slanted toward people who would fit best on the F team. The second half of each question indicates people who would fit best on the P team."

"I can see how those questions help discover whether a person is passionate about the present or the future. How many people do you try to have on each subteam?"

"We try to enlist fifteen people on the vision planning team—fourteen members and one chairperson. The fourteen are then divided into two subteams of seven people each—six members and one leader. It looks like this." Marvin drew the following chart on a piece of paper and handed it to me.

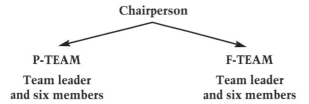

"People agree to serve on the team for at least two years. We do our best to make certain to include some new people in our church on each subteam."

"Now that's dangerous," I said, feeling concern.

"Not really," Marvin assured me. "Our teams are made up of a good balance between newer people and those who have been around a long time. To me that plaque on my wall says it all." It read:

**If you keep thinking
what you've always thought,
you'll keep getting
what you've already got.**

"Having newer people on each of our subteams keeps us from what is called 'groupthink.' Groupthink is the tendency of groups who have been together a long time to think the same. If we are honestly going to continuously improve our current ministry, and dream new dreams for the future, we must allow for new thinking."

Nodding in agreement, I prodded, "I'm really interested in this approach. Give me some more detail as to exactly what each of the subteams does."

"You know," Marvin spoke excitedly, "I thought that would be your next question. Let's look at each subteam separately. The way I see it, the P team asks two main questions: *Where are we?* and *How are we doing?* The F team asks two different questions: *Where are we going?* and *How are we going to get there?* To clarify the difference between the two teams even more, look at this page I've developed for our own subteams."

P Team Asks	F Team Asks
Where are we?	Where are we going?
How are we doing?	How are we going to get there?
What are the church's needs?	What are the community needs?
What needs to be improved?	What needs to be developed?
What are the problems?	What are the opportunities?
How do we train current leaders?	How do we add new leadership?
What are the church demographics?	What are the community demographics?
How do we involve members?	How do we reach new people?
What are the internal issues?	What are the external issues?
What are the rules?	How can we break the rules?
How can we preserve the present?	How can we seize the future?
How can we manage the process?	How can we lead the parade?
What is probable?	What is possible?

| How can we satisfy our members? | How can we amaze our members? |
| How can we fine-tune the ministry? | How can we create a new ministry? |

"Another way to look at these teams," Marvin suggested, "is that the P team seeks a proper view of the present, while the F team seeks a proper view of the future."

"Which of these two teams is the most important?" I wondered out loud.

"They're both important," Marvin answered. "The underlying premise in looking back and leaping forward is that we can focus on the present and the future of our church at the same time. Taking hold of future opportunities and improving present ministries are equally challenging. There are unrealized opportunities in both arenas." Marvin picked up his pad of paper and said, "Look at this chart."

	People Served	People Unserved
Articulated Current Needs	Today's Ministry	Current Unrealized Opportunities
Unarticulated Future Needs	Future Unrealized Opportunities	Future Unrealized Opportunities

"As you can see, the current ministry of most churches only serves those people whose needs have been articulated. There are still some people left unserved, even though we know their needs. In addition there is a vast area of unarticulated future opportunities that are not being served at all."

Breaking in, I asked, "So how do the two subteams come together on the vision planning team?"

"They come together in two ways. First, we sometimes assign one of the teams to a particular project. For instance, we might assign our P team to look at our visitor follow-up process. They would then take a detailed look at how visitors are currently being followed up, perhaps visit other churches to see what they are doing in this area, and then suggest some ways to improve our current process. Of course we could also assign our F team to look at visitor follow-up. However, they would look at the future in an attempt to project how visitors' attitudes might change in the next five to ten years, and then project ideas on how to design a totally new approach to reaching newcomers. In both situations the teams function as project teams focusing on only one segment of our church ministry.

"About every five years we do a complete vision plan for the entire church. In this instance the P team serves a second function by taking an audit of the entire church program and making extended recommendations for improving the entire church ministry. The F team looks at the future and makes broad recommendations on what new forms the church must take on to be effective in the future. In this manner the two subteams serve the large process of vision planning."

"You do vision planning for only five years? Wow! I'd assumed we'd be planning for ten or more years."

"That may have been the case several years ago," Marvin smiled in agreement. "However, we've discovered that things change so rapidly today that a long-range plan for us is about five years out. We do make some general assessments of what might take place ten to twenty years out, but we hold those ideas lightly."

"We've found that the vision planning process helps lift people out of their ruts to begin moving in a new direction," Marvin noted. "I think it's wise to remember that often people think they are in the groove when they are really only in a rut."

I laughed again. "That is so true." I paused to think about what I needed to ask next. And then I remembered to ask about selecting the team.

> **PEOPLE THINK THEY ARE IN THE GROOVE WHEN THEY ARE REALLY ONLY IN A RUT.**

"The selection of the vision planning team is extremely important," Marvin began. "We start by making a long list of people we believe would fit well on this type of team. Then we spend time praying over our list, asking God to direct us to the right people for the team. I like to say that powerful prayer is essential for a powerful plan."

"I've been wondering where prayer fits into the process," I commented. "It seems to me that

> **POWERFUL PRAYER IS ESSENTIAL FOR A POWERFUL PLAN.**

prayer often gets left out of most churches' planning processes."

"That can be true," Marvin agreed, "and we've taken steps to see that prayer remains a vital part of our vision planning, as you'll discover later. Now, as we begin making the actual selection, we look for a number of things. First, we look among the larger congregation for people who have integrity. If the people of the church are going to accept the vision planning team's plan, then the members of the team must be trusted and respected by the entire congregation. Second, we look for broad representation from the congregation. An attempt is made to include people of various ages, experience, length of time in the church, gender, and so on. Third, we always try to include people who have the authority to help carry out the plan. For example, we try to include the chairpersons of the finance committee, our administrative board, and other key teams."

"That makes a lot of sense," I said. "If the key people in the church don't have input into the planning process, the final plan may not be supported."

"Correct!" Marvin seemed pleased that I had grasped this aspect of planning. "Developing ownership of the plan is essential if it is to be carried out later on. Thus key leaders in the church must be on this team. However, I want to suggest two other crucial aspects of organizing the team. We try to recruit at least 20 percent of the people on the team from those who have been in our church for less than two years."

"Isn't that kind of dangerous?" I asked.

"At first glance, it may seem so," Marvin nodded, "but it's been our experience that having 20 percent of the vision planning team as newer members of our church provides for fresh ideas that we wouldn't otherwise enjoy. The newer people cannot overpower the vision team but they do add input that is invaluable to the planning process."

"Umm, I see."

"Another aspect that I should mention relates to generational makeup of the vision planning team. Basically we try to balance the team generationally with the same generational percentage we find in our community."

"I don't understand." I couldn't see what the community had to do with the church's vision planning team.

"It's been our experience that if you want the vision planning team to think evangelistically, you must match the makeup of the team to that of the community. So, if the composition of our community is 20 percent people over sixty years old, 60 percent middle-aged, and 20 percent people under thirty-five years old, we try to reflect the same age-group percentages in our vision planning team."

"I've never heard of this concept before," I admitted.

"Neither had we, but it seemed to make sense so we tried it. We find that by recruiting our people to reflect the age makeup of our community we plan more effectively for outreach into the community."

"Okay, let me summarize," I said. "What you're saying is that I should recruit people who are respected in my church, already hold important offices, broadly represent the people in my church, and reflect the age groups in my community."

"That's correct," Marvin said. "You may not be able to fit all of those guidelines exactly, but that's why they're called *guidelines*. Just do the best you can."

"So after I've put together a vision planning team and divided people into P teams and F teams, what do I do next?"

"A great question. Let's walk down to the coffee shop and talk some more about this."

After taking notes for about an hour, this is what I had in my notebook.

Insights for looking back, leaping forward

- We live life forward by understanding it backward.

- It's important to look both ways down the road.

- The past is for remembering not reliving.

- A good past is the best future. Key Scripture: Joshua 4.

- When you're not sure where you're going, look to where you've been.

- *St. John's Syndrome: the tendency of a church to become less effective as it ages. Key Scripture: Revelation 2-3.*

Assemble the Team

- *TEAM means Together Everyone Accomplishes More.*
- *Divide into a P team and an F team.*
- *P teams focus on improving present ministries.*
- *F teams focus on creating future ministries.*
- *Involve new people: If we always think what we've always thought, we'll always get what we've already got.*
- *Remember: People think they're in the groove when they are really only in a rut.*

5

WHAT WE DO

MISSION

A T 10:30 WE SAT DOWN at a table in the coffee shop of Birkshire Innovations, a small but well-known consulting firm in our city where Marvin Woods works. Once we were seated, Marvin continued our conversation about how to look back and leap forward.

"Once you have your vision planning team in place, you need to develop four statements: a mission statement, a core values statement, a vision statement, and a goal statement."

"You know," I broke in, "I've always been confused as to the difference among those four areas. What's the difference between mission, values, vision, and goals?"

"You're right! They are a little confusing. I've seen people use these terms in various ways. However, I try to think of them like this." Marvin wrote the following on a napkin:

Mission: What we do
Values: What we believe
Vision: What we see
Goals: What we achieve

"Exactly what does that mean?" I asked.

Marvin smiled. "Let's take them one by one. Mission is sometimes referred to as 'purpose.' I don't think it matters which word you use, as long as you are consistent in using the same word. Essentially, mission is the biblical reason your church exists. As such, the mission of your church never changes, and you can never completely accomplish it. For example, here's how my church states it:

**The mission of Grace Church is
to present the gospel to all people and
prepare them to be followers of Jesus Christ.**

"I think you can see that our mission can never be completely fulfilled. As long as there are lost people living without a personal relationship with Christ, and others who need to grow in their walk with Christ, our mission will still be viable."

I nodded as he talked.

"A mission statement should be biblical; that is, it must be founded on the Word of God. My church's mission statement is supported by the Great Commission in Matthew 28:19–20. 'Go therefore and make disciples of all the nations, baptizing them in the name of the Father and the Son and the Holy Spirit, teaching them to observe all that I commanded you; and lo, I am with you always, even to the end of the age.'"

"I've got that. What else?"

"It should define what needs you will minister to rather than what programs you will provide."

"Give me a couple of examples."

Marvin offered the following examples: "A church should move from listing programs in its mission statement to listing the purpose of the programs. Here are a few examples." Marvin wrote the examples on another napkin.

From	To
Offering Sunday school	Educating children
Offering vacation Bible school	Evangelizing children
Offering adult Bible fellowships	Discipling adults
Offering counseling	Caring for hurting people

"A church would do well to change from the first statements to the second ones. None of the first statements are necessarily wrong, of course, but they do not focus on the underlying purpose like the second ones do. As you look back at my church's mission statement, you can see that our basic mission is to prepare people to be followers of Jesus Christ. Our statement focuses on people's need to be followers of Christ. Note that nothing in the statement says how we will do this. We don't list anything that even remotely sounds like a program or ministry."

"I noticed that. It's very short and easy to remember also."

"That's correct! A mission statement should be short—not more than twenty-five words. Ours is only twenty-two words. And we can even say it in a shorter version: The mission of Grace Church is to prepare people to be followers of Jesus Christ. Why, that's only fifteen words. It must be short enough for people to remember."

"But shouldn't it say a little bit more? It almost seems *too* short," I countered.

"I hear you. What we've done at Grace is to have three basic versions of our mission statement. We have a short version, a standard version, and an expanded version. Here they are so you can see how they are developed."

Short Version The mission of Grace Church is to prepare people to be followers of Jesus Christ.

Standard Version The mission of Grace Church is to present the gospel to all people and prepare them to be followers of Jesus Christ.

Expanded Version The mission of Grace Church is to:

present the gospel to people in a way that is . . .

- Creative—using new, innovative methods
- Compelling—in the power of the Holy Spirit
- Caring—within sensitive, compassionate relationships

and to:

prepare them to be followers of Jesus Christ, followers who are . . .

- Committed to the Word—growing in maturity
- Committed to serve—giving in time, talent, and treasure
- Committed to others—caring for one another.

After hearing Marvin explain the three versions of Grace Church's mission statement, I shook my head and said, "Wow! You've really thought this through."

"Certainly! You should know, however, that we try to get our people to remember only the shorter version. I think the expanded version is more like our philosophy of ministry. Our philosophy is to use new, innovative methods, for example."

"So how did you arrive at your mission statement?" I inquired.

"We started with our senior pastor and allowed him to write the original version. Then we passed it around to the leaders and took suggestions on how to revise the statement. Eventually we shared it with most of the congregation to see what they might add. We call this process 'pulsing.'"

"Why *pulsing?*" I asked.

"It's simple, really. We just try to take the pulse of the leaders and congregation at various points in the planning process. Here, let me diagram it for you."

As Marvin drew the diagram, I began to understand the term.

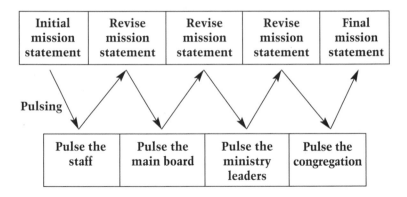

"As you can see, it takes time to pulse the congregation along the way. At each step we take an ever widening pulse of the congregation. However, the advantage is that everyone in the church is given an opportunity to contribute. By the time we go through this pulsing process, there is solid ownership of the final statement among the congregation.

"We did learn two very important facts while developing our mission statement that you should keep in mind as you develop your church's mission statement. First, we learned that mission isn't about us; it's about them. I don't know if it's true, but I've heard there is a maxim in big-game hunting: The larger an animal is, the harder it is to see. Evidently

> **MISSION ISN'T ABOUT US; IT'S ABOUT THEM.**

the animal is so obvious that it is mistaken for something benign and familiar and is missed. The point? We sometimes miss the obvious. It's something like the old adage, 'I can't see the forest for the trees.' We spend a great deal of time missing the obvious. Jesus clearly said, 'For the Son of Man has come to seek and to save that which was lost' (Luke 19:10). Since Jesus is the head of the church, it seems pretty clear that the mission of a local church must reflect his concern for the lost. We tried several different versions of a mission statement before we settled on the one we now have. If we had just taken Christ's mission seriously from the beginning, I think we could have arrived at our statement quicker."

"Thanks for the reminder. Sometimes we do miss the obvious," I said.

Marvin continued, "The second thing we learned is that there is a big difference between having a shared mission and merely having something in common. At first our pastor simply shared the mission statement from the pulpit and hoped people caught the spirit of it. Later we discovered that people couldn't even recall having heard it. We found that we needed to communicate our mission in many different ways. We now have banners hanging in our auditorium that share the mission statement. We print it on all pieces of literature from the church. It is on our business cards, letterhead, and envelopes. Our pastor weaves it into his sermons about every other week so that people will remember it. In short, we do all we can to keep our mission before the people. It's taken about five years, but it is finally getting into the minds and hearts of our people."

THERE IS A BIG DIFFERENCE BETWEEN HAVING A SHARED MISSION AND MERELY HAVING SOMETHING IN COMMON.

"I'm surprised that it takes that much effort to help people remember a mission statement. It's really very short."

"I know but I'm only sharing what I've seen in our church," Marvin assured me. "You see, the problem is not just getting people to remember the mission statement; it's getting them to own it! We found that our people had a lot in common, but getting them to have a 'shared mission' meant going to a higher level. A good illustration of what we're trying to develop is seen in the early church in Jerusalem. Two times it is said of the first church that they had 'one mind' (Acts 1:14; 2:46), and once it is said that they were of 'one heart and soul' (Acts 4:32). We want our people to be of one soul, heart, and mind when it comes to the mission statement."

"I guess having a mission statement is no quick fix," I said earnestly. "Why do you think it takes so long to capture the hearts of people?"

"There are likely a lot of different reasons, but part of the problem is the large amount of information people have to be aware of today. We are literally bombarded with input from all directions. Some say we have several thousands of messages directed at us each day! Fortunately God has built into our minds filters that keep most of this information out. It takes repetition to overcome the natural barriers.

"Another reason is that the natural process of communication creates loss at every level on the communication chain. Here's what I mean. Look at this chart."

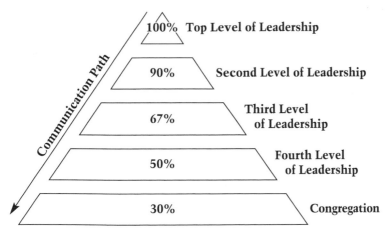

"At the top level, the mission is shared with an expectation that the people will remember 100 percent of it. As you can see, the second level of leadership actually catches only about 90 percent of it.

57

As the mission is communicated farther down the various levels of church leadership, more and more of it is lost until fewer and fewer people understand it. At the third tier of leadership, only about 67 percent of the message is heard. By the fourth tier, only 50 percent is received. When the communication reaches the congregation, only about 30 percent of the message is received."

"Why does the top level of leadership understand the mission better than the bottom level?" I asked.

"It's just the way the natural process of communication goes," Marvin explained. "Have you ever played a game at a party where a person whispers something in the ear of a second person? The message is whispered in the ear of another person and so forth until it gets to the last person? When the last person receives the message, he or she shares it with the entire group."

"Right! And the message is never the same, is it?"

"Never!" Marvin agreed. "For some reason, when a message is passed along, a certain percentage is lost in the translation. The farther along the message is passed, the larger a percentage is lost. This is why it takes repetition of the mission for good communication to take. Each time it is shared, more of the message is remembered. This is why commercials on television or the radio are repeated so often. The first time you hear a commercial for a fast-food restaurant, for instance, you won't remember much about it. But after you've heard the commercial over and over, you're singing their song."

"If I understand what you're saying, a church must communicate its mission over and over until the people are singing it. Right?"

"Correct!"

"So . . . where do we go from here?"

"I'd say we should go for lunch. How about you?"

"That sounds good. I'm hungry."

"Good. I hope you like Mexican food. There's a great Mexican restaurant right around the corner."

"That will be fine."

My notebook was continuing to grow. It now contained the information below.

Insights for looking back, leaping forward

- We live life forward by understanding it backward.

- It's important to look both ways down the road.

- The past is for remembering not reliving.

- A good past is the best future. Key Scripture: Joshua 4.

- When you're not sure where you're going, look to where you've been.

- St. John's Syndrome: the tendency of a church to become less effective as it ages. Key Scripture: Revelation 2-3.

Assemble the Team

- TEAM means Together Everyone Accomplishes More.

- *Divide into a P team and an F team.*

- *P teams focus on improving present ministries.*

- *F teams focus on creating future ministries.*

- *Involve new people: If we always think what we've always thought, we'll always get what we've already got.*

- *Remember: People think they're in the groove when they are really only in a rut.*

Determine Your Mission

- *It tells what we do.*

- *It is the biblical reason our church exists.*

- *It should be shorter than twenty-five words.*

- *It isn't about us; it's about them.*

- *It must be communicated regularly to capture the heart and soul of our people.*

6

WHAT WE BELIEVE

VALUES

I TOOK THE LIBERTY OF INVITING LaVerne Thomas to have lunch with us today," Marvin said as we sat down at our table in the restaurant. "She's a very active member of our vision planning team, and I thought you'd enjoy hearing her viewpoint on remembering values."

It wasn't long before LaVerne joined us. After a brief time of casual conversation to get acquainted, LaVerne asked, "So what have you two discussed so far?"

"We spent a good deal of time discussing how to organize the vision planning team into P teams and

F teams earlier this morning, and just before lunch we talked about defining a church's mission," Marvin summarized. "I think we're ready to talk about a church's core values."

"I assumed that's why you invited me along for lunch. Holding on to our core values is a major concern of mine," LaVerne admitted. "You see, I've been afraid that with all of the innovations taking place in churches, we may be eroding the values that set the church apart in the first place."

"I've had some similar concerns myself," I quickly agreed.

"I think a lot of people are fearful about the loss of traditional values in our society. It's one thing to see values eroded on television, but it's quite another to see them eroded at church!" LaVerne exclaimed.

"Hmm," reflected Marvin, "I hear what you're both saying but I think we have to be cautious that we don't put an unrealistic perspective on the past. I remember a cartoon I saw a number of years ago that featured the apostle Paul. In the cartoon he has just finished writing the Book of 1 Corinthians, and he expresses his fear that even though he addressed such problems as gluttony, party spirit, incest, and other issues that someday people will look back on it all as the 'good old days.'"

"The good old days weren't always so good, were they?" I laughed along with Marvin and LaVerne.

"No, they were not," Marvin affirmed. "Pastor Bob pointed out a Bible verse that says it well. It's found in Ecclesiastes chapter seven, verse ten: 'Do not say, "Why is it that the former days were better than these?" For it is not from wisdom that you ask about this.' The good old days were never as good as we think they were. In fact I've been told that the only reason we think the past was so good is that, as we grow older, the number of things that annoy us increases."

"What do you mean?" LaVerne asked.

"When we were children, we didn't pay much attention to bad things. We focused on playing and really didn't think much about the news of wars in other countries, murders taking place in our own cities, or people deceiving others. Only when we became adults did we begin to notice such happenings. The world has always had its share of problems; we just weren't aware of them when we were young. Thus we tend to think of the years when we were younger as being the good ones. The truth is they were never quite as good as memory tells us. Remember: There is no better way to waste time in life than to dwell on the past. We should learn from the past with as much objectivity as possible, and then move on."

> THERE IS NO BETTER WAY TO WASTE TIME IN LIFE THAN TO DWELL ON THE PAST.

"I see what you mean," I said. "But how do past values fit in?"

"Values are the constant in the midst of change," Marvin explained. "The methods by which we do ministry change over time, but the values remain the ties to the past and the future. The way I like to illustrate it is by thinking of a hot-air balloon. I'm not an artist, so cut me some slack. Look at this sketch."

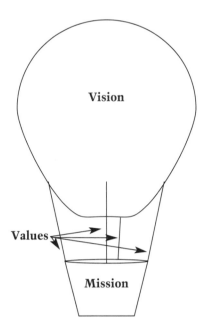

"We talked about it this morning: The mission is the biblical reason we exist as a church. The mission is illustrated in my sketch by the basket in which people ride. If you've ever seen a hot-air balloon, you've probably noticed that the baskets on all the balloons look pretty much the same. In the same sense, the mission statements of various churches are much the same. Of course, they may be stated differently, but a close look will reveal they are very similar. For instance, I used to attend a church that said its mission was to know Christ and make him known. A few years later, I attended a church that said its mission was to win people to

Christ and build them up in the faith. These two churches stated their mission differently, but essentially they were the same."

"I see what you mean," I agreed.

"The vision is illustrated in this sketch by the balloon. The vision of churches will vary greatly, sort of like the colors and designs of hot-air balloons. We'll talk more about the vision later. However, as you can see, the lines that tether the basket to the balloon are the values. What I'm attempting to picture is that the values of a church are what tie mission and vision together. As we seek to move forward using new methods and ministries, the values keep us tied to our mission. Obviously, if a hot-air balloon didn't have the tethers connecting the basket and the balloon together, the basket wouldn't get off the ground. This is the situation many churches find themselves in. They may have developed a mission statement and a vision statement, but without tying them all together with their values, nothing works."

LaVerne jumped in. "Fortunately, the process of looking back and leaping forward provides a way to keep moving forward by building on our past values, rather than losing them, or, as Marvin suggests, keeping our mission and vision tied together with our core values."

"So what exactly are core values, and how do I find them?" I asked.

"Core values are what a church stands for or holds dear," she began.

Marvin added, "They are the heart and soul of the church."

"Agreed," LaVerne said. "Additionally I'd say they are the beliefs on which we make decisions; or perhaps another way to say it is they are what's really important."

"The problem," Marvin pointed out, "is that values are usually unwritten and unrecognized. They are what we call 'tacit' values, that is, unwritten values."

"Correct," LaVerne agreed. "When we first started to define our values, we had a difficult time figuring out what they were. We knew they existed, and had a major role in decision making, but we couldn't seem to find a way to state them."

"So what did you do?" I asked.

"We found a creative tool that helped our people identify our core values. By using our church name as an acrostic," Marvin said, "we discovered that our people were able to verbalize ingrained values of our church. Here. Look at this card."

Marvin handed me what looked like a credit card, but it had the following printed on it.

Grace Church

Our Mission:

To prepare people to be followers of Jesus Christ

Our Values:

Genuine Christian Living
Reaching the Lost
Authentic Worship
Continuous Growth
Excellence in Ministry

"As you can see," Marvin explained, "our values are listed as an acrostic of our name. We are strongly committed to the authority of Scripture and believe the Bible reveals the person of God and how we should live our Christian lives. Our aim is to present the claims of Jesus Christ in ways that will effectively reach our postmodern society. Thus we see our core values under five major headings. Our first core value is genuine Christian living. To us that means we will seek to disciple our people into deeper relationships of honesty, love, and service. The second value is reaching the lost. We believe it is crucial to use as many means as possible to reach people for Christ, because lost people matter to God. Our third value is authentic worship. We believe that God is worthy of worship, and we want to give him praise. Our fourth value is continuous growth. To us growth has a twofold dimension: quality and quantity. We believe we are called to assist our people in developing a biblical worldview that affects their beliefs, values, and behaviors. But we also believe we must find and fold the lost into our church body. Our fifth and last core value is excellence in ministry. We believe we must do the best we can with what God has given us. That's where looking back and leaping forward are so important. We must have continuous improvement, as well as continuous growth."

"Using an acrostic," LaVerne affirmed, "really was a key to surfacing our core values."

Interrupting, I asked, "It's creative, but tell me specifically the steps you used to arrive at the final version of the acrostic."

Looking across the table at Marvin, LaVerne waited for him to answer. He motioned for her to go ahead. "The first thing we did was ask people to give us a list of the values they thought we should hold on to no matter what. We started with the senior pastor, then took his list to the main board, and asked them to add to it. Then we compiled their answers into sort of a revised version and handed it out to all of our ministry leaders, asking them to add to it. Once the vision planning team received all of their replies, we took the entire list and revised it again. We kept careful track of the statements or phrases that were mentioned numerous times. On occasion we had to do some interpreting. For instance, some people listed Sunday school, Sunday evening worship, and vacation Bible school as values. We felt those were programs, rather than values, but we tried to find the hidden value beneath the program. In our conversations we determined that in the minds of our people, Sunday school expressed the value of education, or as we stated it, continuous growth. The value beneath Sunday evening worship we decided was fellowship, which we stated as genuine Christian living. The underlying value of V.B.S. was outreach, which we stated as reaching the lost. It took the vision planning team about three months to develop the acrostic you now see."

LaVerne looked at Marvin and said, "Marvin, why don't you tell Wendy how we communicate the values to our people?"

"We already talked some about the need for communication earlier this morning when we discussed the mission statement," Marvin recalled. "I'd say that you need to communicate the values in similar ways. Perhaps something we didn't talk about, which would be important to highlight here, is the need to align values and ministries."

"Yes, that would be a good idea," LaVerne agreed.

"The principle to keep in mind incorporates our look-back-leap-forward idea: We look back to find our values; we leap forward to find our methods."

"Tell me more about aligning values and ministries," I requested.

"Perhaps an illustration would help. When we first began talking about looking back and leaping forward, a large number of our people assumed that meant we would revive former programs or

> **WE LOOK BACK TO FIND OUR VALUES; WE LEAP FORWARD TO FIND OUR METHODS.**

ministries. We had canceled our Sunday evening worship service about five years before we began the look-back-leap-forward process. At the time of canceling the service, we had more than two hundred adults attending on Sunday morning but only about twenty adults coming on Sunday evenings. It just came to the place where it wasn't practical to continue the evening service. Later, when we began the process of looking back and leaping forward, many assumed we would revive the old Sunday evening worship service. The purpose of looking back, however, is to discover the values beneath the old programming, not to revive the old programming. Fortunately our church leaders understood the principle that we look back to find our values; we leap forward to find our methods."

"What the leaders did," LaVerne explained, "was to develop a new small-group ministry on Sunday evenings, built on the core values of the past. The leaders determined that the core value beneath the evening worship service was fellowship, or genuine Christian living. In addition, other values represented in the evening worship service were authentic worship and continuous growth. Rather than simply trying to revive the old method of Sunday evening worship, the leaders looked forward for a new method that would fulfill the same values, but be culturally relevant to today."

"That's right," Marvin added. "What they finally chose to do was to begin a small-group ministry on Sunday evenings in the homes of various members. Small-group ministry carries on the core values of the former Sunday evening worship service, but furthers them in a way that is relevant to today's church members. You see, small groups allow for fellowship, or genuine Christian living, authentic worship, and continuous growth."

"And you know what happened?" LaVerne interjected. "The small groups attracted nearly 120 people! We went from only 20 people attending Sunday evening worship to 120 people participating in small groups on the same evening."

"It worked," Marvin suggested, "because we looked back to identify the core values of Sunday evening worship, but then leaped forward to find a new method that would carry on those core values."

"Let me give you an example of something we're doing right now that is based on the same process," LaVerne volunteered. "I've worked in V.B.S. for nearly twenty-five years. Why, I can remember when we had more children attend our two-week V.B.S. than attended on an average Sunday morning. However, a few years ago we noticed that fewer and fewer children were taking advantage of this ministry. So we began the look-back-leap-forward process. First, we looked back to identify the core values of V.B.S. After talking with people who had been involved with V.B.S. for many years, we determined that the core value of V.B.S. for our church was evangelism. We then leaped forward to see if there was a new way we could evangelize children that would be effective today. What we discovered is that youth soccer has become a major activity in our community.

"One of our fathers brought us some research that confirmed more children are participating in youth soccer in our city than in any other activity. After doing some investigating, we also found out that several of our members are already coaching youth soccer. The short story is we are not going to do a traditional V.B.S. this coming summer. Instead, we are going to offer a weeklong soccer camp from 9:00 A.M. to 1:00 P.M. Monday through Saturday. The camp will focus on teaching children soccer skills, but during their break times and at lunch, one of the coaches will be telling a Bible story, and one of the coaches will be sharing his or her testimony with the children. An invitation will be given each day for children to accept Christ as their personal Savior. On Saturday all of the parents of the children will be invited to attend a demonstration of what the children have learned: They'll play a short soccer game and end with a barbecue lunch. All parents will be given a packet of information on soccer skills, but the packet will also include information on how to become a believer in Christ, as well as information on our church's ministry. Also, during the day, one of the coaches will share a testimony of faith in Christ, and another will tell how to become a Christian."

"I see what you're doing," I noted. "You are carrying on the core values of V.B.S. but using a new method, or ministry, that is relevant to children and parents today."

"I think she's got it," Marvin confirmed, smiling at LaVerne.

"Yes, she does," LaVerne agreed, "and I've got to get going. I just noticed the time. Thanks for lunch. It was great getting to know you, Wendy."

"Bye," I waved as LaVerne left the table.

"I think we need to get back to the office," Marvin said as he rose from the table. "When we get back, let's talk about vision."

"Okay," I mumbled as I finished writing in my notebook. Here is what I had written.

Insights for looking back, leaping forward

- We live life forward by understanding it backward.
- It's important to look both ways down the road.
- The past is for remembering not reliving.
- A good past is the best future. Key Scripture: Joshua 4.
- When you're not sure where you're going, look to where you've been.
- St. John's Syndrome: the tendency of a church to become less effective as it ages. Key Scripture: Revelation 2-3.

Assemble the Team

- TEAM means Together Everyone Accomplishes More.
- Divide into a P team and an F team.
- P teams focus on improving present ministries.
- F teams focus on creating future ministries.
- Involve new people: If we always think what we've always thought, we'll always get what we've already got.
- Remember: People think they're in the groove when they are really only in a rut.

Determine Your Mission

- It tells what we do.
- It is the biblical reason our church exists.
- It should be shorter than twenty-five words.
- It isn't about us; it's about them.
- It must be communicated regularly to capture the heart and soul of our people.

Remember Your Values

- Values tell us what we believe.
- Values are the heart and soul of our church.
- Values link us to our past and future by connecting our mission and vision together.
- Using the church's name as an acrostic is a good tool to help people verbalize otherwise tacit values.
- Key principle: We look back to find our values; we look forward to find our methods.

7

WHAT WE SEE

Vision

I AM INTRIGUED WITH YOUR HOT-AIR balloon sketch," I said on entering Marvin's office.

"How's that?" he replied.

"It appears you are saying that vision is what gets the church up in the air. But, at first, I thought it was the mission."

"You're a quick study," Marvin affirmed my insight. "Most people think that once they have developed a mission statement, and communicated it to their people, it will solve all their problems. Unfortunately, as important as the mission statement is, it will not lift the church. Only the vision can do that. Mission tells the beginning of things:

what we are to do. Vision tells the end of things: how we are to undertake God's mission.

"Let me explain it this way." Marvin looked out his office window as though daydreaming as he talked, but I found his thoughts insightful. "Like most people, my wife and I have bills we must pay each month. We save our money and pay our bills, but it's not very exciting to do it. On the other hand, a few years ago we dreamed of taking a vacation trip to Hawaii with some close friends. After talking it over with our friends, we decided to go for it, set a date about two years away, and began saving our money for our dream vacation. We saved our money to pay for our dream vacation and the saving was enjoyable."

"My husband and I are saving for a dream vacation right now," I said. "We never had a real honeymoon but we're saving money each month so we can take our dream honeymoon in a few years."

"It's fun to save for a dream, isn't it? The point I'm trying to make is this. Mission is like saving money to pay bills. It's something we need to do, but it's not always that exciting. Vision is like saving money for a dream vacation. It's something we find exciting to do."

"I hear what you're saying, but I must admit I'm still not sure I understand the difference," I confessed.

"Look at it this way. Mission tells us 'why,' and vision tells us 'what.' Perhaps this will help clarify what I'm saying," Marvin offered. "When I first came to my church, Pastor Bob preached regularly on our mission statement. I found that people understood it fairly well. People understood 'why' we were a church. However, people didn't get involved, few were giving regularly to the offerings, and the general morale was low. The problem was they didn't understand the 'what.'"

"I've been to your church a few times," I mentioned, "and I've noticed that people are highly involved in your church today. What has made the difference?"

"Simply put, the difference is that Pastor Bob casts a vision now rather than just teaching about the mission. As you know, our mission is to 'present the gospel to all people and prepare them to be followers of Jesus Christ.' It's a very biblical and solid statement. It's easy to remember. Unfortunately it doesn't pack any energy because it doesn't call us to do anything specific. Remember this: Nothing becomes dynamic until it becomes specific."

"I'm still lost," I said.

"Okay. Imagine yourself sitting in our congregation when the pastor preaches on our mission statement. As he concludes, he gives an invitation for people

> **NOTHING BECOMES DYNAMIC UNTIL IT BECOMES SPECIFIC.**

in the congregation to make commitments. He might say something like, 'God calls you to make a commitment of your time, money, and energy to help fulfill our mission. Why not make a personal commitment today?' What are you thinking as you sit in the congregation?"

"I'd be wondering what specific ministry or program I'm committing myself to, I guess."

"Exactly," Marvin said. "Even though you would agree with the mission statement, you wouldn't know what you were committing yourself to. Thus you'd be asking the question, *Give my time, money, and energy to what?*"

"I'm beginning to get the picture now. The energy comes from knowing specifically 'what' we will be doing to fulfill our mission."

"Right," Marvin affirmed. "What if the pastor painted a picture of an exciting vision for you? For instance, the pastor might say something like this, 'You all know our mission is to present the gospel to all people. Today I want to share with you a vision of how we are going to reach people right here in our own city. We have acquired a new video on the life of Jesus that has proven to be effective in reaching people. The video has been field-tested in other cities similar to ours, and we feel it will be an excellent tool for us to use in reaching people in our city for Christ. Our vision is to place a copy of this video in every home in our city within the next two years. Yes, this is a big challenge, and we'll need all of you to take part in fulfilling this vision for it to happen. *What can I do?* you ask. I'm glad you asked that question. The videos cost $1.50 each, and we'll need 12,000 videos at a total cost of $18,000. Perhaps some of you could give financially toward the purchase of these videos. We will also need 150 people who will dedicate themselves to delivering one video a week for forty weeks of each of the next two years. Perhaps you could volunteer to deliver some videos to your neighbors. In addition, we need 100 prayer intercessors to pray one hour a week for the homes receiving the videos. Perhaps you could join a prayer intercession team.'"

"Stop. Stop!" I put my hand up. "I'm ready to join up now," I laughed.

"You feel the difference, don't you?" Marvin asked. "Remember: Mission tells us what to do, but vision helps us see it.

> **MISSION TELLS US WHAT WE DO, BUT VISION HELPS US SEE IT.**

"In my example the pastor painted a picture of a vision to help the people see what they were being asked to commit themselves to. It's the seeing of the vision that creates the lift to get the church moving in a new direction. Let's add the following to my sketch of the hot-air balloon."

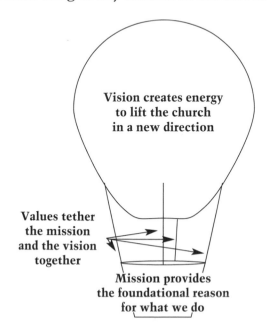

Vision creates energy
to lift the church
in a new direction

Values tether
the mission
and the vision
together

Mission provides
the foundational reason
for what we do

79

"The key to empowering a church in a new direction is having a powerful vision that attracts the big three: time, talent, and treasure. People commit to vision not to mission."

> **PEOPLE COMMIT TO VISION NOT TO MISSION.**

"Now I'm really interested in this aspect," I said. "What other creative ideas can you give me to help me understand vision?"

"Well," Marvin said, "we all live under the same sky, but we don't all have the same horizon. Let me tell you a legend I heard many years ago to illustrate what I mean by that," Marvin suggested.

"Once upon a time there lived a king who was growing old. He knew the time was coming when he would need to give the rule of his kingdom to one of his four sons. The question was, *To which son should he give his kingdom?* To answer that question, the king called his four sons together and gave them a challenge.

> **WE ALL LIVE UNDER THE SAME SKY, BUT WE DON'T ALL HAVE THE SAME HORIZON.**

"'I want each of you to go on a long journey,' the king said. 'While you are on your journey, look for a gift to bring me that will be worthy of my kingdom. Whoever brings me the best gift will receive my kingdom.'

"Taking up the challenge, the first son left on his journey. After a while he came to the Impenetrable Forest. He spent a long time looking for a way through the forest but could not find a way. However, while looking at one of the trees, he noticed one of the limbs was twisted in an unusual manner. He decided to cut down that branch and make it into a cane for his father. *Surely, this will be a gift worthy of a kingdom*, he thought.

"The second son also began his journey. He too came to the Impenetrable Forest, but somehow found a way through. However, farther on, he arrived at the Uncrossable River. After spending some time attempting to ford the river, he gave up. By chance he peered into the river and noticed a sparkling stone. Reaching into the river to retrieve the stone, he realized that he had found a valuable gem. *Surely this will be a gift worthy of a kingdom*, he thought.

"Eventually the third son started on his journey. He too came to the Impenetrable Forest and found a way through. He came to the Uncrossable River and found a way across. But he eventually came to the Unclimbable Mountain. He walked around the base of the mountain looking for a way to the top, but did not find a path. While looking for it, he noticed some flowers, the likes of which he had never seen before. He decided to bundle the roots of the flowers and take them back to make a beautiful flower garden for his father. *Surely this will be a gift worthy of a kingdom*, he thought.

"The fourth son soon began the journey and, like the others, came to the Impenetrable Forest, the Uncrossable River, and the Unclimbable Mountain. But, unlike the others, he found a way through the forest, across the river, and up to the top of the mountain. As he stood on the top of the mountain, he looked to the other side and saw a luscious green valley with streams of crystal clear water. The one thing he could not find, however, was a gift for his father that would be worthy of a kingdom. Sadly, he returned to his father's kingdom.

"After the sons returned, they presented their father with the gifts they hoped would be worthy of a kingdom. The last son had no gift to give but told of the green valley on the other side of the mountain with the crystal clear water. As he described the green valley, he suggested that the people of the kingdom could journey there in the future and live in beauty and peace.

"The following day the father called his sons together. He thanked the first three sons for their gifts, but to the fourth son he gave his kingdom.

"Why did he give the fourth son the kingdom? Because that son gave his father the greatest gift of all—the gift of vision. The father realized that his fourth son had seen a better future for his people. Perhaps the fourth son could lead the people of the kingdom to the green valley with crystal clear water where they would experience a better life."

I nodded. "I like that story," I said. "I read in a magazine recently that leadership is not about managing people; it's more about inspiring them. Would you agree with that?"

"Definitely," Marvin assured me, "and it is vision that inspires, not mission. The job of all leaders is to expand the visionary horizons of their people. The way to do that is to envision a better future, like the fourth son in my story, and lead people in the direction of it."

"How long does it take for church members to catch the vision?" I wondered.

"Here is another chart that will help answer that question," Marvin said as he showed me the following.

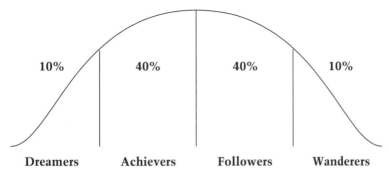

10%	40%	40%	10%
Dreamers	**Achievers**	**Followers**	**Wanderers**

"When an attempt is made to cast a vision to the people, they naturally fall into four groups. The first is the Dreamers. Ten percent of the people generally fall into this group, and they grasp the vision very early on, usually within three to six months. Most important, however, is that they see the vision and then help others to see it and do it.

"The second group is called Achievers. Forty percent of the people will eventually find their way into this group. They are the

> **LEADERSHIP IS NOT ABOUT MANAGING PEOPLE; IT'S MORE ABOUT INSPIRING THEM.**

ones who see the vision and do it. It may take as long as eighteen months for some of them to catch the vision, but when they do, they're on the team. The third group is called Followers. They mirror the size of the Achievers with about 40 percent of the people. It takes most of them two to three years to catch on to the vision. Unfortunately, even after they see it, they are often content to let others do it. The last group is called Wanderers. They match the Dreamers in size and never seem to buy into the vision. They never see it."

> **HAVING A VISION DOES NOT GUARANTEE SUCCESS IN REACHING IT, BUT YOU DON'T HAVE A CHANCE WITHOUT ONE.**

"Based on this chart, I'd guess it takes at least two years to get enough people on board with a vision to move forward."

"It depends somewhat on the size of the vision. If you are going to distribute videos to all the people in your city, as in my earlier story, you might be able to get people to buy into it sooner. If you were trying to help people see a vision to relocate your church, however, it probably would take much longer. Sometimes what may seem like a simple thing—changing a church's name, for instance—will take an extremely long time. I know of one church that took eleven years to change its name! This I know for sure: Having a vision does not guarantee success in reaching it, but you don't have a chance without one.

"Do you still have that plastic card I gave you with our mission and values printed on it?" Marvin asked.

"Yes, I do."

"Turn it over and look on the back. It will give you an example of our vision."

Here is what I read on the back of the card.

Our Vision

To build a loving church family in the midst of broken relationships we will . . .

- Relocate to a new campus in five years
- Build a new multipurpose facility
- Have 50 percent of our people using their gifts
- Get 80 percent of our people into small groups
- Place a Bible in every home in our city

As I read the card, Marvin pointed out, "The vision is very specific, which is why it is dynamic."

I put the card back in my folder. "I have a lot more questions but I think I've taken up enough of your time today," I said.

"I've had a good time talking with you, Wendy. I hope it's been helpful."

"It has been. I plan on talking to at least one more member of your vision planning team sometime next week. Do you have any suggestions who would be the best person to contact?" I asked.

"I recommend you call Sam and Lois O'Conner. They will give you some ideas on how we set goals, overcome obstacles, and put it all together."

"Great. I'll give them a call tonight and set something up for next week," I said as I stood and shook hands with Marvin.

"Two more thoughts," Marvin looked straight in my eyes as he spoke. "First, the best way to predict

> **THE BEST WAY TO PREDICT THE FUTURE IS TO CREATE IT YOURSELF THROUGH A BIG VISION.**

the future is to create it yourself through a big vision. And second, don't sacrifice your values; you'll always lose."

"Wow, I have a lot to think about," I said. "Thank you so much for your time today. I've been on a real learning curve."

"You're welcome. Feel free to call me anytime if I can help."

"You can count on it!"

> **DON'T SACRIFICE YOUR VALUES; YOU'LL ALWAYS LOSE.**

Later that evening, I took a few moments to fill in my notebook with some new ideas. Here is what I've now written down.

Insights for looking back, leaping forward

- We live life forward by understanding it backward.

- It's important to look both ways down the road.

- The past is for remembering not reliving.

- A good past is the best future. Key Scripture: Joshua 4.

- When you're not sure where you're going, look to where you've been.

- St. John's Syndrome: the tendency of a church to become less effective as it ages. Key Scripture: Revelation 2-3.

Assemble the Team

- TEAM means Together Everyone Accomplishes More.

- Divide into a P team and an F team.

- P teams focus on improving present ministries.

- F teams focus on creating future ministries.

- Involve new people: If we always think what we've always thought, we'll always get what we've already got.

- Remember: People think they're in the groove when they are really only in a rut.

Determine Your Mission

- It tells what we do.

- It is the biblical reason our church exists.

- It should be shorter than twenty-five words.

- It isn't about us; it's about them.

- It must be communicated regularly to capture the heart and soul of our people.

Remember Your Values

- Values tell us what we believe.

- Values are the heart and soul of our church.

- Values link us to our past and future by connecting our mission and vision together.

- Using the church's name as an acrostic is a

good tool to help people verbalize otherwise tacit values.

- *Key principle: We look back to find our values; we look forward to find our methods.*

Dream a New Dream

- *Key principle: People commit to vision not to mission.*

- *We all live under the same sky, but we don't have the same horizon.*

- *Having a vision does not guarantee success in reaching it, but you don't have a chance without one.*

- *The best way to predict the future is to create it yourself through a big vision.*

- *Don't sacrifice your values; you'll always lose.*

8

WHAT WE ACHIEVE
GOALS

I CALLED SAM AND LOIS O'CONNER to set up a time to meet and discuss how to "set goals, overcome obstacles, and put it all together," as Marvin had suggested. As it turned out, they invited me over to their house for lunch. I was fortunate my husband was able to take a personal day off from his work to watch our children so that I could spend an afternoon with Sam and Lois. While we ate lunch, I shared my tale of seeking to learn how to look back and leap forward. As I finished, I asked, "What do you suggest are the next steps?"

"Once you've determined your mission, vision, and values," Sam said, "I'd recommend that you develop specific goals, or steps, that will guide your direction."

"Sounds good to me," I agreed. "How do I begin?"

"Have you heard of the Nine Pregnant Women rule?" asked Lois.

Laughing a little, I admitted I had not heard of such a rule.

"Well," Lois continued, "it takes nine months to have a baby—but you can't get the job done in one month with nine pregnant women. It takes time for the natural process to develop! This rule applies to any project. After writing your mission, vision, and values, it's critical that you identify which steps you must complete sequentially over the necessary period of time it will take to accomplish your vision."

"And those steps are called goals," Sam added.

"Yes," Lois quickly jumped back into the conversation. "Goals are the steps that must be completed to reach the vision."

> THINK BIG; START SMALL.

"Correct," Sam agreed. "And we like to say, Think big; start small. It's necessary to think big about your vision, but it's equally important to start small by setting some reachable and controllable goals."

"Didn't you say Marvin gave you a balloon sketch that shows how the elements of the planning process work together?" Lois asked.

"Yes, he did."

"Let's see if we can add a new dimension to it," Lois suggested.

After I found it in my notebook, this is what Lois and Sam added.

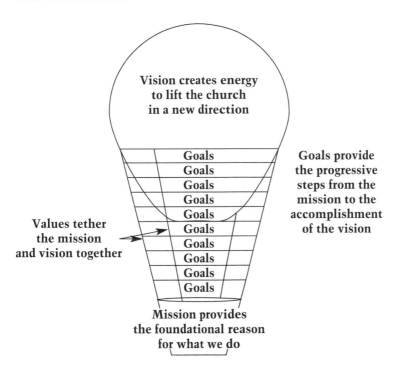

"The goals serve as steps to move from the mission to the accomplishment of the vision," Sam explained. "The goals are like lines that tie the mission, vision, and values all together. As each of the goals is achieved, we get closer to the accomplishment of the mission and vision."

"It's all becoming much clearer," I said. "I've had some experience setting goals. I head up one of my church's children's departments. Each year we review what we accomplished and didn't accomplish in the last twelve months. Then we set goals for the next year based on what is left over from the last year and add a few new goals."

"That's how most churches set their goals," Lois agreed, "but there is a better way to do it."

"We've found that there are two types of goals," Sam interjected, "survival goals and mission goals. For example, when a church focuses on what hasn't happened in the past, it's developing survival goals. However, when a church focuses on what can happen in the future, it is developing mission goals. Over the last few years I've developed a chart that I think you'll find helpful in understanding the difference between survival goals and mission goals," Sam commented as he handed me a copy of his chart.

Survival Goals	Mission Goals
1. Focus on what has not happened	1. Focus on what can happen
2. Produce remedial solutions	2. Produce innovative solutions
3. Based on the past	3. Based on the future
4. Doubt based	4. Dream based
5. Identify problems	5. Identify potentials
6. Lower congregational morale	6. Raise congregational morale
7. Demand low level of faith	7. Demand high level of faith

"We've discovered that it's best to look at the mission and dream big about what God wants us to do in the future," Sam continued. "So, rather than building on what we didn't accomplish last year, we basically begin over each year and think about what God wants us to do in the coming year. Financial planners call this zero-based budgeting; that is, you zero out last year's budget and begin from scratch to build a new budget for the coming year. I guess you could call ours a zero-based goal-setting process. We zero out last year's goals and set new goals for the next year."

"Okay, I see what you mean. So how do you go about it?"

"First, we organize a team with three people from each area of church ministry, for example, worship, adult education, facilities, and so forth. Second, we provide each team with a copy of our mission, vision, and values. Then we ask each team to meet with other people from their area of ministry and develop as many goals as they can think of that God might want them to accomplish in the coming five to ten years. We expect them to have basic goals—like reviewing curriculum—and long-term goals—like hiring a new staff member. We ask them to dream big dreams and not to limit their thinking of what God might want for their area of ministry. Someone once remarked that when it comes to goals we should shoot for the moon. Even if we miss it, we will end up among the stars.

> **SHOOT FOR THE MOON. EVEN IF YOU MISS IT, YOU WILL END UP AMONG THE STARS.**

"Each team must come up with a minimum of nine goals, but if they have more that's great. Of course, all of their goals must contribute in some way to accomplish our overall mission and vision, as well as remaining true to our core values."

"My first thought is that you'll have way too many goals," I commented.

"You're right," Lois agreed. "So we help them narrow their goals to what must be accomplished in the short term, mid term, and long term."

Sam continued, "We're getting a little ahead of ourselves. Let's back up a step or two. After the various teams put together their lists of goals, then we schedule an 'open-space' planning meeting."

"What's an open-space meeting?" I asked.

"It's a way to create excitement and inspiration among everyone to accomplish the mission and vision of a church," Lois emphasized.

"Here's how we hold the open-space meeting," Sam kept talking. "We find a room large enough for everyone to fit into and we remove all of the furniture except folding chairs. A fellowship hall, gym, or other similar room works very well. The chairs are arranged in a circle so people can see each other. After all the participants arrive, the leader gives a short opening statement about our mission, vision, and core values, reminding everyone in attendance that whatever goals we arrive at must fit these key guidelines for our church ministry. Sheets of easel paper and marking pens are distributed to each team, and then the teams are dismissed to different locations in the room. They carry their chairs to a wall or corner of the room and reconvene their team. After each team regroups, their job is to take all of the goals they have, plus any new ones they may think of, and prioritize them into short-range, mid-range, and long-range goals."

I wrote this down in my notebook. Then I looked up and asked, "What time lengths do you assign to short-range, mid-range, and long-range?"

"Good question," Sam said. "Any goal that can be accomplished in less than two years is considered short-range. Goals that will take between three and five years to complete are mid-range. Anything that takes longer than five years is a long-range goal."

While I continued to write in my notebook, I nodded and said, "Go on."

"The teams debate the order of priority for all of their goals and write them on the blank sheets of easel paper. As each team completes its prioritized list, they tape their sheets of paper on one of the walls in the room. A break is taken for refreshment and fellowship. After the break, the entire group comes back together and someone from each ministry team reads and explains to the larger group the team goals. All of the participants are encouraged to ask questions and make suggestions for all areas of ministry. The open-space meeting with the entire group encourages everyone to look at all the goals with fresh eyes and to offer suggestions. We've discovered that some of our breakthrough ideas come from people outside of a particular ministry."

"The entire open-space planning meeting usually takes from three to five hours," Lois said. "When all the teams have had an opportunity to share their goals and answer questions, then the meeting is over. However, sometimes we have 'breakout groups' that continue to develop their goals. For instance, if one of the ministry teams is wrestling with determining its goals, they may continue to meet as a breakout group. When this happens, anyone from the larger group who wishes to stay and help is free to do so. Others can leave if they desire."

"Later on," Sam continued, "each team turns in its list of goals to the chairperson of the planning team. The chairperson puts all of the goals together into a rough-draft long-range plan."

"Do you have a sample I can see?" I asked.

"Yes. I don't have a copy of our church's entire plan but Lois and I are on the worship ministry team and I have a copy of our church's worship goals."

Here is a copy of what Sam gave me.

Worship Goals

Short-range (1–2 years)   *Target Date*
- Train prayer counselors for   May 4
  worship prayer time.
- Purchase a PowerPoint projector.   June 1
- Fine-tune guest registration   September 15
  procedure.

Mid-range (3–5 years)

- Recruit a drama team and begin a drama ministry.
- Place sound baffles in the worship center to dampen noise.

- Install new carpet in the worship center to update style and color.

Long-range (6–10 years)

- Develop and use videos in worship service.
- Hire a worship arts pastor.
- Purchase a new sound system.

"So what's next?" I asked as I studied the list of goals.

"The vision team meets to go over the rough draft of goals. All of the goals are evaluated against the following three questions:

- Do the goals sustain the mission of our church?
- Do the goals move us toward our vision?
- Do the goals uphold our core values?

"Of course, each ministry's goals are specifically designed for that ministry. However, all of the goals must help move the church toward its larger mission and vision," Sam explained. "Additional goals are added from the P team and the F team to round out the entire plan."

"We also plan time lines on each goal," Lois added. "Our pastor says that goals are dreams with deadlines. As you can see

> **GOALS ARE DREAMS WITH DEADLINES.**

from the worship goals Sam gave you earlier, target dates have been set for all the goals in the short-range category."

"Why don't you set dates for the mid-range and long-range goals?" I asked.

"We used to," Sam said, "but we found through trial and error that things are changing so fast in today's world that it didn't help to set dates beyond one or two years. Since we set our goals each year, the ones in the mid-range and long-range categories are often moved up to short-range during our next planning session."

"Or," Lois interrupted, "they'll be dropped entirely. You see, sometimes we set mid-range and long-range goals only to discover that God leads us in a different direction later on. We try to remain flexible to the leading of the Holy Spirit, while at the same time maintaining a sense of direction. The Bible verse that directs us in this process is Proverbs 16:9, 'The mind of man plans his way, but the LORD directs his steps.' We feel God wants us to plan a direction, but to be flexible enough to change directions as he leads us."

> IF YOU DON'T KNOW WHERE YOU'RE GOING, YOU'LL END UP SOMEPLACE ELSE.

"That reminds me of what that famous theologian Yogi Berra once said," Sam laughed. "He reportedly said, 'If you don't know where you're going, you'll end up someplace else.'"

"Yogi Berra, a theologian?" I smiled. "So how do you handle obstacles to your goals?"

"Let's adjourn to the family room for dessert before we get into that topic," Lois suggested.

Sam directed me to the family room. Then he and Lois cleared the table and prepared the dessert. I took the opportunity to look over the notes I had taken during our conversation. The following is what I have noted so far.

Insights for looking back, leaping forward

- We live life forward by understanding it backward.

- It's important to look both ways down the road.

- The past is for remembering not reliving.

- A good past is the best future. Key Scripture: Joshua 4.

- When you're not sure where you're going, look to where you've been.

- St. John's Syndrome: the tendency of a church to become less effective as it ages. Key Scripture: Revelation 2-3.

Assemble the Team

- TEAM means Together Everyone Accomplishes More.

- Divide into a P team and an F team.

- P teams focus on improving present ministries.

- F teams focus on creating future ministries.

- Involve new people: If we always think what we've always thought, we'll always get what we've already got.

- Remember: People think they're in the groove when they are really only in a rut.

99

Determine Your Mission

- It tells what we do.
- It is the biblical reason our church exists.
- It should be shorter than twenty-five words.
- It isn't about us; it's about them.
- It must be communicated regularly to capture the heart and soul of our people.

Remember Your Values

- Values tell us what we believe.
- Values are the heart and soul of our church.
- Values link us to our past and future by connecting our mission and vision together.
- Using the church's name as an acrostic is a good tool to help people verbalize otherwise tacit values.
- Key principle: We look back to find our values; we look forward to find our methods.

Dream a New Dream

- Key principle: People commit to vision not to mission.
- We all live under the same sky, but we don't have the same horizon.
- Having a vision does not guarantee success in reaching it, but you don't have a chance without one.

- *The best way to predict the future is to create it yourself through a big vision.*

- *Don't sacrifice your values; you'll always lose.*

Set Some Goals

- *Think big; start small.*

- *Develop mission goals not survival goals.*

- *Use a zero-based goal-setting process.*

  Organize a team of three people for each ministry.

  Have the team develop potential goals.

  Host an open-space meeting.

  Sort goals into short-range, mid-range, and long-range.

- *Shoot for the moon. Even if you miss it, you will end up among the stars.*

- *Goals are dreams with deadlines.*

- *If you don't know where you are going, you'll end up someplace else.*

9

OVERCOME OBSTACLES

"EVERYTHING WE'VE TALKED ABOUT today certainly hits home with me," I said as Lois handed me a plate with a large piece of apple pie.

"What do you mean?" Sam asked.

"Our entire conversation on setting goals," I explained. "I've set goals in the past, but I can see now that they've always been survival goals rather than mission goals."

"I'm glad to know we've been helpful to you, Wendy," Lois said. "It sounds like you're really wrestling with how to look back and leap forward."

"Indeed I am. I guess I'm like many other people who set goals. It's exciting to develop the goals, but then I always seem to run into obstacles that keep me from reaching them."

"Overcoming obstacles is just part of life," Sam advised. "Sometimes the obstacles are real, while other times they are just our perceptions. A few years ago, I was driving an unfamiliar road, almost late for an appointment. Up ahead of me I saw a train apparently blocking the road. Fearing that a delay would make me late, I began to look for alternate roads, but finding none, I continued toward the train. As I got closer, I realized the train was on an over-pass, and the road that seemed to be blocked went under the train. Had I tried other roads, I would have surely been late. I learned an important lesson that day that many times obstacles in the distance seem impassable, but when we persevere, they disappear."

> **MANY TIMES OBSTACLES IN THE DISTANCE SEEM IMPASSABLE, BUT WHEN WE PERSEVERE, THEY DISAPPEAR.**

"I've had similar experiences myself," I said.

"We all have, I think. Sometimes the obstacles are real. One aspect of leadership is learning how to see the real obstacles early on and devise a plan to overcome them."

"You've hit on the main issue for me," I confessed. "One of the reasons I've been reluctant to take on the job of chairperson of my church's vision planning team is a lingering frustration I have from serving on ineffective committees. Many of the plans and goals I've seen developed in past committees were never fulfilled. I'm just too busy to spend time serving on a vision planning team that doesn't produce something worthwhile."

"I think you're like a lot of people today," Lois agreed. "From what I've read, most people have less than three hours to devote to ministry outside of Sunday morning worship."

"That's right," Sam added. "People in our church are very selective regarding service in ministry or on a committee. That's why it's so important to have a clear statement of mission, vision, and values. People must sense their service is of real value to the overall direction of the church's ministry."

"You'll get no argument from me on that point," I assured Sam and Lois.

"But let me encourage you not to be afraid of setting goals," Sam advised. "Remember: If you push the limits today, you do what was impossible yesterday.

> IF YOU PUSH THE LIMITS TODAY, YOU DO WHAT WAS IMPOSSIBLE YESTERDAY.

"What you have to learn is to employ the four principles of alignment. I call them the four Ms of alignment," Sam noted.

"The four Ms of alignment," I echoed as I once again took out my notebook.

"The four Ms of alignment are the ingredients for overcoming barriers to your goals. Highly successful leaders employ these four Ms with great consistency."

"What are they?" I asked eagerly.

"Let me have your notebook," Sam continued, "and I'll write them down for you."

I handed Sam my notebook and he wrote:

The Four Ms of Alignment

Manpower
Money
Management
Ministry of Prayer

"Before we talk about the four Ms of alignment," I said as Sam handed my notebook back, "tell me what you mean by *alignment*."

"It's really quite simple," Sam began, "but also easily missed. Let me put it this way: Alignment is the intentional organizing of a church's practices and behaviors so that they're consistent with its stated goals, values, vision, and mission.

"The biggest obstacle to seeing your church's goals fulfilled is misalignment. A church can set wonderful goals, but if the church's organization does not align in support of the goals, most will fail."

"So what you're saying," I summarized, "is that the main obstacle to overcome in reaching our goals is internal rather than external."

"Yes," Sam answered. "As you can see, the first principle of alignment is *manpower*. The manpower of the church must be deployed to fulfill its goals, values, vision, and mission. This is clearly an internal issue. One of the main obstacles to overcome in reaching goals is the lack of people support. For a goal to be accomplished, it must have sufficient people devoting their talents and energies to seeing it fulfilled. When a church sets a goal, it must ask, *How can we make sure people are working toward the achievement of this goal?* If you can't align people with the goal, there's a high probability it will not be reached."

"So sufficient manpower must be in place for a goal to succeed," I said. "What about the second principle of alignment—*money?*"

> **ALIGNMENT IS THE INTENTIONAL ORGANIZING OF A CHURCH'S PRACTICES AND BEHAVIORS SO THAT THEY'RE CONSISTENT WITH ITS STATED GOALS, VALUES, VISION, AND MISSION.**

"We don't like to talk about money too much in churches," Lois said, "but the reality is we can't do much without it. Not only must sufficient manpower be deployed but adequate money must be used to fulfill the church's goals, values, vision, and mission. This is where the budget of the church comes into play. A church must ask the question, *Is the budget supporting the accomplishment of the church's goals?* Someone once remarked that we can tell our priorities by looking at our checkbooks. The same can be said for our church. What does our church's checkbook say about its commitment to its goals, values, vision, and mission? When it comes to goals, we must remember that the cost of doing nothing is greater than the cost of doing something."

"That's really getting to the bottom of things," I replied. "From a personal point of view, I know my husband and I evaluate our financial commitments on a regular basis. I guess it's important for a church to do the same."

> THE COST OF DOING NOTHING IS GREATER THAN THE COST OF DOING SOMETHING.

"Yes, it is," Lois remarked. "One of the major obstacles to overcome in reaching goals is the lack of financial support. A few years ago we became concerned that our church was not effectively reaching new people for Christ. Someone suggested we find out how much money we were spending on outreach to our local community. We were shocked to discover that in our entire budget of $189,000 only $500 was going toward outreach. Our money was not aligned with our evangelistic goal. When you develop your plans, be sure to think about how you'll align the church's finances to support your goals."

"That's good advice that I'll try to remember. Now tell me about *management*, the third principle of alignment."

"Management," said Sam, "is the time issue. The management of the church's calendar should be designed to fulfill its goals, values, vision, and mission. As we discussed earlier, people have only so much time to devote to ministry today. Thus wise church leaders will carefully plan the church's calendar so that it directs people toward fulfillment of its goals rather than away from them. Church leaders should ask the question, *Does our calendar of events reflect our goals, values, vision, and mission?"*

"Think of it this way," Lois suggested. "If the average person gives only three hours to church activities beyond the Sunday worship service, then we need to be certain the opportunities for service we offer point us in the direction of our goals, values, vision, and mission."

"I think this is why so many people today don't come out to everything the church offers," Sam said. "Years ago it was a common practice for people to attend church every time the doors of the church were open."

"My grandmother reminds me of that whenever I see her," I laughed.

"I'm sure she does," Sam laughed with me. "But there is so much more competition for our time today that people must of necessity make choices. People are astute enough to see that some events the church offers are not as strategic as others."

"I know what you're saying," I confirmed. "My husband and I used to attend Sunday evening worship services until we had children. Lately we've felt it's more important to our family to stay home on Sunday evenings. Being together is a high value to us as a family and we just felt we were spending too much time separated at church. We still feel a little guilty about not going on Sunday evenings."

"Especially when you see your grandmother, I bet," Lois laughed.

"Right!"

"One of the reasons churches are streamlining their programming is related to this principle of alignment," Sam explained. "Time is so valuable today that an effective church must carefully align its programming so that it supports its goals."

"So . . ." I looked at my notebook. "The fourth principle of alignment is *ministry of prayer*. Tell me about that."

Lois answered this time. "We like to say, when you make your way, put the Maker in it. A church's ministry of prayer should be carried out to fulfill its goals, values, vision, and mission. Now, all churches pray, but most do not strategically pray in a way that aligns their prayer ministry with the goals of the church. For example, how many churches have prayer intercessors specifically aligned to pray for worship, or facilities, or youth, and so on? I think one of the reasons our church has done so well in reaching its goals is that we actually recruit people to pray specifically in line with our goals, values, vision, and mission."

> **WHEN YOU MAKE YOUR WAY, PUT THE MAKER IN IT.**

"Can you give me more of an example?" I asked.

"Here's the rest of the Worship Goals sheet," Sam said, handing me another sheet of paper.

Alignment

Manpower:	Bill S. will train prayer counselors.
	Bob R. will purchase a PowerPoint projector.
	Mary W. will develop a new registration procedure.
Money:	$100 is budgeted for training prayer counselors.
	$7,500 is budgeted for a PowerPoint projector.
	$500 is budgeted for a new registration process.
Management:	Prayer counselors will serve in only one service a month.
	Bob R. has full authority to purchase a projector.
	Mary W. is relieved of other responsibilities.
Ministry of Prayer:	Prayer counselors will hold a quarterly prayer retreat.
	Sam and Lois O. will pray for Bob's purchase of projector.
	Mary W. to recruit a prayer team for new guests.

"As you can see," Lois continued, "we have attempted to think through each of the four Ms so that they are aligned with our goals. By doing this, we are addressing the major obstacles ahead of time."

> **THE MANPOWER QUESTION: IS THE MANPOWER OF OUR CHURCH DEPLOYED TO FULFILL OUR GOALS?**
>
> **THE MONEY QUESTION: IS THE MONEY OF OUR CHURCH USED TO FULFILL OUR GOALS?**
>
> **THE MANAGEMENT QUESTION: IS THE SCHEDULE OF OUR CHURCH DESIGNED TO FULFILL OUR GOALS?**
>
> **THE MINISTRY OF PRAYER QUESTION: IS THE PRAYER OF OUR CHURCH CARRIED OUT TO FULFILL OUR GOALS?**

"Over the last few years, we've found that goals can be stopped by the simplest things," Sam shared. "One of the stories our pastor likes to tell is about African gazelles. According to him, the African gazelle can leap thirty feet horizontally and ten feet vertically. Yet it can be easily kept in any enclosure with a wooden or solid fence only three feet high. Gazelles will not jump over anything, unless they can easily see exactly where their feet will land. The pastor's question to us is, *What are the three-foot fences that hold us in?* In most situations our controlling fences, or obstacles, can be addressed by answering the manpower, money, management, and ministry of prayer questions.

"It may be helpful to think of these four Ms in different terms," Sam continued. "For example, you may prefer asking if your goals are aligned with the congregation (manpower), checkbook (money), calendar (management), and contemplation (prayer). Or you could use the words talent, treasure, time, and trajectory. Let me write these in your notebook," Sam suggested. Here is what he wrote:

Manpower=Congregation=Talent
Money=Checkbook=Treasure
Management=Calendar=Time
Ministry of Prayer=Contemplation=Trajectory

"This is all very helpful," I said. "I've never considered the necessity of aligning these aspects of ministry to advance our goals."

"Most people haven't," Lois replied, "and that's one reason goals don't get accomplished."

"I like to think of it like this," Sam said. "Don't be discouraged just because there's a fence on this side of the pasture. The gate may be open on the other side."

"Sam's always coming up with these aphorisms," Lois said; then

> DON'T BE DISCOURAGED JUST BECAUSE THERE'S A FENCE ON THIS SIDE OF THE PASTURE. THE GATE MAY BE OPEN ON THE OTHER SIDE.

she added, "But I guess they do make a point." She smiled. "There are two other obstacles that we often face when setting goals that you should be aware of. First, goals need to be controllable."

"I don't understand," I interjected. "I thought goals were to stretch our faith."

"That's true," Sam said, "but we need to set goals that are controllable. Let me give you an example.

The first time I served on our planning team I was on the evangelism council. We set a goal to win one hundred people to Christ in twelve months. Now that's a fine goal, but the truth is we can't control what other people do. The goal is not controllable and it sets us up for failure right from the beginning.

"We discovered it was better to write the goal in a manner that we could control. In our research we found that 12 percent of the people who visited our church ended up receiving Christ as their Savior. Using that percentage as our guideline, we determined that we needed to attract twelve hundred new people to church in twelve months to see one hundred people come to Christ. So we set a goal of inviting twelve hundred guests to attend our church in twelve months, or one hundred guests per month. We could control that goal by developing ways to attract that many guests to church."

> **GOD WANTS BOTH OUR PRAYER AND OUR PARTICIPATION.**

"I'm understanding it now," I said. "It obviously still takes faith to see one hundred people come to Christ, but you state the goal in a way that you can do some planning from your end toward its accomplishment."

"You've got it," Sam affirmed. "You see, God wants both our prayer and our participation. Paul tells us in 1 Corinthians chapter three, verse six, 'I planted the seed, Apollos watered it, but God made it grow.' I like to say it this way: Without God we cannot do anything; without *us*, God *will* not do anything. God certainly doesn't need us but he chooses to work through us.

> **WITHOUT GOD, WE CANNOT DO ANYTHING; WITHOUT *US*, GOD *WILL* NOT DO ANYTHING.**

"Second, your goals need to be reachable. We sincerely believe we can reach one hundred new people for Christ in one year's time. If, on the other hand, we had said one thousand people, it wouldn't have been realistic. A goal needs to be large enough to stretch the faith of your people without discouraging them."

"That's important to keep in mind," I agreed.

While Sam and Lois cleaned up our dessert plates, I took a few moments to jot down some additional thoughts in my notebook. From all my interviews, I had amassed quite a number of ideas.

Insights for looking back, leaping forward

- *We live life forward by understanding it backward.*

- *It's important to look both ways down the road.*

- *The past is for remembering not reliving.*

- *A good past is the best future. Key Scripture: Joshua 4.*

- *When you're not sure where you're going, look to where you've been.*

- *St. John's Syndrome: the tendency of a church to become less effective as it ages. Key Scripture: Revelation 2–3.*

Assemble the Team

- TEAM means Together Everyone Accomplishes More.

- Divide into a P team and an F team.

- P teams focus on improving present ministries.

- F teams focus on creating future ministries.

- Involve new people: If we always think what we've always thought, we'll always get what we've already got.

- Remember: People think they're in the groove when they are really only in a rut.

Determine Your Mission

- It tells what we do.

- It is the biblical reason our church exists.

- It should be shorter than twenty-five words.

- It isn't about us; it's about them.

- It must be communicated regularly to capture the heart and soul of our people.

Remember Your Values

- Values tell us what we believe.

- Values are the heart and soul of our church.

- Values link us to our past and future by connecting our mission and vision together.

- Using the church's name as an acrostic is a

good tool to help people verbalize otherwise tacit values.

- Key principle: We look back to find our values; we look forward to find our methods.

Dream a New Dream

- Key principle: People commit to vision not to mission.

- We all live under the same sky, but we don't have the same horizon.

- Having a vision does not guarantee success in reaching it, but you don't have a chance without one.

- The best way to predict the future is to create it yourself through a big vision.

- Don't sacrifice your values; you'll always lose.

Set Some Goals

- Think big; start small.

- Develop mission goals not survival goals.

- Use a zero-based goal-setting process.

    Organize a team of three people for each ministry.

    Have the team develop potential goals.

    Host an open-space meeting.

    Sort goals into short-range, mid-range, and long-range.

117

- *Shoot for the moon. Even if you miss it, you will end up among the stars.*

- *Goals are dreams with deadlines.*

- *If you don't know where you are going, you'll end up someplace else.*

Overcome Obstacles

- *Remember: If you push the limits today, you do what was impossible yesterday.*

- *The four Ms of Alignment*

  Manpower

  Money

  Management

  Ministry of Prayer

Definition: Alignment is the intentional organizing of a church's practices and behaviors so that they're consistent with its stated goals, values, vision, and mission.

Principle: The cost of doing nothing is greater than the cost of doing something.

- *Questions to address obstacles*

  The manpower question: Is the manpower of our church deployed to fulfill our goals?

  The money question: Is the money of our church used to fulfill our goals?

The management question: Is the schedule of our church designed to fulfill our goals?

The ministry of prayer question: Is the prayer of our church carried out to fulfill our goals?

Manpower=Congregation=Talent

Money=Checkbook=Treasure

Management=Calendar=Time

Ministry of Prayer=Contemplation= Trajectory

- *Don't be discouraged just because there's a fence on this side of the pasture. The gate may be open on the other side.*

10

PUT IT TOGETHER

IT DID NOT TAKE LOIS AND SAM long to put the dessert dishes away. I had offered to help, but they told me to just take my time writing down my thoughts in my notebook. By the time they finished in the kitchen, I had finished entering my notes. As they came back into the family room, I said, "The time has gone very fast today."

"Yes," Sam agreed. "But we'd like to talk about putting it all together. Do you have time?"

"Oh, yes," I said. "That would be most helpful. I understand the basic steps for looking back and leaping forward, but how does it all fit together?"

"Let's look at this from different directions," Sam suggested. "The end product of the look-back-leap-forward process is a written plan for the future of the church's ministry. The plan is based on the mission, vision, and values of the church. Its development takes into serious consideration both the past history of the church and its future opportunities. Later we'll give you a complete copy of our plan for your files. You'll need time to digest this."

"In some ways the planning process is more important than the end product," Lois suggested.

"Exactly," Sam continued. "Let me try to explain the road we took to get to where we are. One of the key elements in helping a church develop one mind and heart for the future is to help the people go through the process together."

Lois explained, "In our church we like to say that a successful plan will be P.O.L.S. This acrostic means the following. The *P* equals the Purpose of the church. Under purpose we include our mission, vision, and values. The purpose must come first for an effective ministry. The *O* equals Organization. Under organization are the two Ms: money and ministry of prayer. Next is *L*, which stands for Leadership. Of course, this relates to manpower. Finally, *S*, which stands for Supervision or management."

"We feel that it's crucial to develop a long-range plan in the exact order of P.O.L.S.," Sam added. "A few years ago we tried doing it backward, but it didn't work. It actually turned out so awful that we now say, If you do it backwards you'll get S.L.O.P."

"There you go again," Lois teased.

"I think our pastor has a better way of illustrating the process," Sam noted. "Let me draw you a picture."

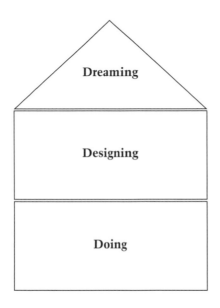

"Our pastor views the church as a three-story building. The top floor is for *dreaming*. It's at this level that the mission, vision, and values of a church are developed. The second level is for *designing*. It's at this second level that the short-range, mid-range, and long-range goals are developed. The lower level is for *doing*. It's at this level that the actual work of ministry is done."

"Maybe it would help if you expanded on the picture a little more, Sam," Lois encouraged.

"As you'll note, the dreaming level covers the entire structure. You might think of it as the roof of a house. The roof covers the house, providing protection and a unity of structure. Thus the mission, vision, and values of a church provide a covering for all of a church's ministries."

"Dreaming is mainly the responsibility of the senior staff and the major board of a church," Lois added. "In our church we've found the dream needs to be revisited about every three to five years."

"Let's add that to my drawing," Sam said.

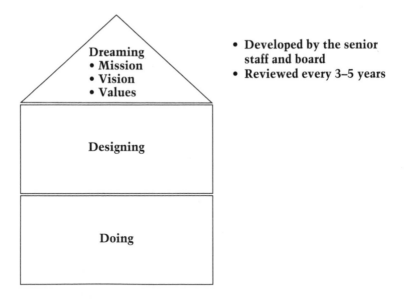

"The designing level is where the ministries of a church are to be found. In larger churches the various ministries are usually led by staff members. In smaller churches there is a committee, or perhaps board members, assigned to each area of ministry. As you can see from the drawing, all of the ministries fit under the roof of the building; that is, they build toward the mission, vision, and values of the total church. The ministries I've listed are just a sample of what many churches do. The idea is that each of them must contribute in some manner to the mission, vision, and values of the total church. It's at this level that the goals are developed for each area of ministry. In addition, the P teams and F teams function at this level," Sam said.

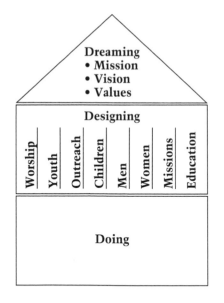

- Developed by the senior staff and board
- Reviewed every 3–5 years

- Developed by the associate staff and committees
- Reviewed every year

"The bottom floor is where the day-to-day, week-to-week, and month-to-month ministry takes place," Lois noted. "That is why we call it the 'doing' level. Most of a church's volunteers and support staff are located on this level. Let me add some more to our drawing."

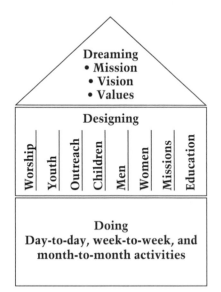

- Developed by the senior staff and board
- Reviewed every 3–5 years

- Developed by the associate staff and committees
- Reviewed every year

- Done by volunteers and support staff
- Reviewed weekly and monthly

"It's pretty clear that the process for looking back and leaping forward begins at the top and works its way toward the bottom. Am I correct on this?" I asked.

"You are correct," Lois confirmed. "First, a church looks back to identify its mission and values. Second, it develops a vision for the future based on those criteria. Third, a church establishes goals that will take it step by step toward its mission, vision, and values. Last, a church aligns the four Ms so that the day-to-day work of the church supports the overall mission, vision, values, and goals. As an example, here is a complete copy of our current plan for the worship ministry of our church. We call it 'Charting Our Future.'"

Charting Our Future
A Worship Ministry Plan for Grace Church

Our Mission (What we do . . .)
The mission of Grace Church is to prepare people to be followers of Jesus Christ.

Our Mission Expanded (How we'll do ministry . . .)
Grace Church exists to *present* the gospel to people in a way that is

- Creative—using new, innovative methods
- Compelling—in the power of the Holy Spirit
- Caring—within sensitive, compassionate relationships

and to *prepare* them to be followers of Jesus Christ, followers who are
- Committed to the Word—growing in maturity
- Committed to serve—giving in time, talent, and treasure
- Committed to others—caring for one another

Our Vision (What we see . . .)
While mending broken relationships, we the people of Grace Church have a vision to build a strong and loving church. To accomplish this vision we will

- Relocate to a new campus within five years
- Build a new multipurpose facility within ten years
- Involve 50 percent of our people in the use of their spiritual gifts
- Get 80 percent of our adult worshipers into small groups
- Place a Bible in every home in our city within five years

Our Values (What we believe . . .)

The values that tend to drive our ministry are

Genuine Christian living

Reaching the lost

Authentic worship

Continuous growth

Excellence in ministry

Our Worship Goals

Short-range (1–2 years)   *Target Date*

- Train prayer counselors for   May 4
worship prayer time.
- Purchase a PowerPoint projector.   June 1
- Fine-tune guest registration   September 15
procedure.

Mid-range (3–5 years)

- Recruit a drama team and begin a drama ministry.
- Place sound baffles in the worship center to dampen noise.
- Install new carpet in the worship center to update style and color.

Long-range (6–10 years)

- Develop and use videos in worship service.
- Hire a worship arts pastor.
- Purchase a new sound system.

Alignment

Manpower: Bill S. will train prayer counselors.

Bob R. will purchase a PowerPoint projector.

Mary W. will develop a new registration procedure.

Money:	$100 is budgeted for training prayer counselors.
	$7,500 is budgeted for a PowerPoint projector.
	$500 is budgeted for a new registration process.
Management:	Prayer counselors will serve in only one service a month.
	Bob R. has full authority to purchase a projector.
	Mary W. is relieved of other responsibilities.
Ministry of Prayer:	Prayer counselors will hold a quarterly prayer retreat.
	Sam and Lois O. will pray for Bob's purchase of projector.
	Mary W. to recruit a prayer team for new guests.

"Each area of ministry has its own specific plan," Lois reminded me, "and each plan is formulated in the same manner as our worship plan."

"I'm surprised at all the hard work that goes into formulating such a plan," I admitted.

"That's true," Lois agreed. "After years of looking back and leaping forward, we've found that it takes a lot of unspectacular preparation to produce spectacular results."

"If you'll allow me to offer one last tidbit before we finish," Sam interjected, "I advise: Prepare yourself for opportunities; then let those opportunities find you."

> **PREPARE YOURSELF FOR OPPORTUNITIES; THEN LET THOSE OPPORTUNITIES FIND YOU.**

"Like I told you, Wendy. He's always coming up with these!"

"Well," I said, "after listening to all your ideas, I have a new aphorism for you: Look back in satisfaction, look forward in anticipation."

"That's good," Lois said and Sam nodded.

Then I added, "I've found all your comments extremely helpful."

> **LOOK BACK IN SATISFACTION; LOOK FORWARD IN ANTICPATION.**

"So, after all the research you've done in the last two weeks," Sam asked, "are you going to accept the position as chairperson of your vision planning team?"

"I'm not sure. I'll take some time to talk with my husband about it and I'd appreciate your prayers for me as I make my final decision."

"We'll certainly be praying for you. In fact let us pray for you now before you go."

The time with Sam and Lois had helped me understand how to set goals, overcome obstacles, and put it all together. As I sat in the car in front of their house I jotted down a few final thoughts in my notebook. By now, my notebook had grown considerably. Here is what it looks like.

Insights for looking back, leaping forward

- *We live life forward by understanding it backward.*

- *It's important to look both ways down the road.*
- *The past is for remembering not reliving.*
- *A good past is the best future. Key Scripture: Joshua 4.*
- *When you're not sure where you're going, look to where you've been.*
- *St. John's Syndrome: the tendency of a church to become less effective as it ages. Key Scripture: Revelation 2-3.*

Assemble the Team

- *TEAM means Together Everyone Accomplishes More.*
- *Divide into a P team and an F team.*
- *P teams focus on improving present ministries.*
- *F teams focus on creating future ministries.*
- *Involve new people: If we always think what we've always thought, we'll always get what we've already got.*
- *Remember: People think they're in the groove when they are really only in a rut.*

Determine Your Mission

- *It tells what we do.*
- *It is the biblical reason our church exists.*
- *It should be shorter than twenty-five words.*
- *It isn't about us; it's about them.*

- It must be communicated regularly to capture the heart and soul of our people.

Remember Your Values

- Values tell us what we believe.

- Values are the heart and soul of our church.

- Values link us to our past and future by connecting our mission and vision together.

- Using the church's name as an acrostic is a good tool to help people verbalize otherwise tacit values.

- Key principle: We look back to find our values; we look forward to find our methods.

Dream a New Dream

- Key principle: People commit to vision not to mission.

- We all live under the same sky, but we don't have the same horizon.

- Having a vision does not guarantee success in reaching it, but you don't have a chance without one.

- The best way to predict the future is to create it yourself through a big vision.

- Don't sacrifice your values; you'll always lose.

Set Some Goals

- Think big; start small.

- *Develop mission goals not survival goals.*
- *Use a zero-based goal-setting process.*

  Organize a team of three people for each ministry.

  Have the team develop potential goals.

  Host an open-space meeting.

  Sort goals into short-range, mid-range, and long-range.

- *Shoot for the moon. Even if you miss it, you will end up among the stars.*
- *Goals are dreams with deadlines.*
- *If you don't know where you are going, you'll end up someplace else.*

Overcome Obstacles

- *Remember: If you push the limits today, you do what was impossible yesterday.*
- *The Four Ms of Alignment*

  Manpower

  Money

  Management

  Ministry of Prayer

Definition: Alignment is the intentional organizing of a church's practices and behaviors so that they're consistent with its stated goals, values, vision, and mission.

133

Principle: The cost of doing nothing is greater than the cost of doing something.

- Questions to address obstacles:

  The manpower question: Is the manpower of our church deployed to fulfill our goals?

  The money question: Is the money of our church used to fulfill our goals?

  The management question: Is the schedule of our church designed to fulfill our goals?

  The ministry of prayer question: Is the prayer of our church carried out to fulfill our goals?

  Manpower=Congregation=Talent

  Money=Checkbook=Treasure

  Management=Calendar=Time

  Ministry of Prayer=Contemplation=Trajectory

- Don't be discouraged just because there's a fence on this side of the pasture. The gate may be open on the other side.

Put It Together

- A successful plan is P.O.L.S.

  P=Purpose: Mission, Vision, and Values

  O=Organization: Money and Ministry of Prayer

L=Leadership: Manpower

S=Supervision: Management

- *View the church as a three-story house.*

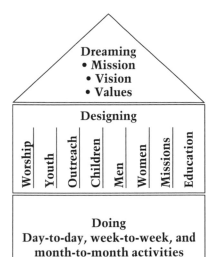

- Developed by the senior staff and board
- Reviewed every 3–5 years

- Developed by the associate staff and committees
- Reviewed every year

- Done by volunteers and support staff
- Reviewed weekly and monthly

- *Prepare yourself for opportunities; then let opportunities find you.*

POSTSCRIPT

A S I DROVE THE LAST FEW BLOCKS to my church, my mind kept slipping back to the people I had met with during the last few weeks. It was enjoyable to get to know each person, but even more important, I appreciated the way they helped me learn to look back and leap forward.

Pastor Steve and I are going to meet in fifteen minutes, and I know he will be anxious to hear my decision concerning the chairperson position. My husband and I have spent the last few days discussing and praying about my role on the vision planning team. You cannot imagine how thankful I am to have such an understanding and supportive husband. While I sometimes doubt my own abilities, he is so encouraging. After all the prayer, discussions, and interviews, I think that my ability to build a team is just what our church needs on its vision planning team. So, as you may have guessed,

> **IT TAKES A STEP BACKWARD TO REMIND US OF WHAT'S REQUIRED TO MOVE AHEAD.**

I have chosen to accept the chairperson position.

Of course, it took a little longer to make this decision than I had expected. However, one thing I have learned is that sometimes it takes a step backward to remind us of what's required to move ahead.

ABOUT THE AUTHOR

DR. GARY L. MCINTOSH is a nationally known author, speaker, educator, consultant, and a professor of Christian Ministry and Leadership at Talbot School of Theology, Biola University, in La Mirada, California. He has written extensively in the field of pastoral ministry, leadership, generational studies, and church growth.

Dr. McIntosh received his B.A. in Biblical Studies from Colorado Christian University, an M.Div. in Pastoral Studies from Western C.B. Seminary, and a D.Min. in Church Growth Studies from Fuller Theological Seminary.

As president of The McIntosh Church Growth Network, a church consulting firm he founded in 1989, Dr. McIntosh has served more than 500 churches in 53 denominations throughout the United States and Canada. The 1995 and 1996 president of the American Society for Church Growth, he edits both the *Church Growth Network* newsletter and the *Journal of the American Society for Church Growth*.

Services Available

Dr. Gary L. McIntosh speaks to numerous churches, organizations, schools, and conventions each year. Services available include keynote presentations at major meetings, seminars and workshops, training courses, and ongoing consultation.

For a live presentation of the material found in *Look Back, Leap Forward* or to request a catalog of materials or other information on Dr. McIntosh's availability and ministry, contact:

The McIntosh Church Growth Network
P.O. Box 892589
Temecula, CA 92589-2589
909-506-3086

On the World Wide Web at:

www.mcintoshcgn.com

or

www.churchgrowthnetwork.com

SAMYA JOHNSON

THE SIMPLE TRUTH

The Quran and the Bible Side-by-Side

The Simple Truth: The Quran and the Bible Side-by-Side
Copyright 2013 by Call of Love Ministries Publications

Graphic design and layout by: Laura Brown
Cover image photo credit: jocic/shutterstock

ISBN-10: 0-9890913-0-9
ISBN-13: 978-0-9890913-0-5

Versions of the Quran used are:
Abdullah Yusuf Ali, The Holy Qur'an: Translation and Commentary, Lahore, Pakistan, 1934.
Saheeh International, The Qur'an: English Meanings and Notes, Riyadh: Al-Muntada Al-Islami
    Trust, 2001-2011; Jeddah: Dar Abul-Qasim 1997-2001.
Pickthall, Muhammad Marmaduke William, The Meaning of the Glorious Qur'an, London, 1930.
Ghali, Muhammad Mahmoud, Towards Understanding the Ever-Glorious Qur'an, Cairo, 2003,
    originally published 1997.

For more information, or to order additional copies (bulk pricing available) contact:
Call of Love Ministries
Tel: 832-220-4040
Email: info@calloflove.org
Web: calloflove.org
P.O. Box 498698
Cincinnati, OH 45249 USA

Table of Contents

PURPOSE AND USE:

This book is intended for both Christians and Muslims alike. It was written with a younger generation in mind.

This volume is not comprehensive, but it is intended to be used as a quick reference or guide. For additional resources and references please visit calloflove.org.

The capitalization in the Quran verses were copied exactly as they appear in versions sited.

Subjects are presented in alphabetical order for ease of searching.

Islam has different sects. Some minority sects may not hold to certain practices or doctrines mentioned.

This book is available as both an e-book and in paperback.

Bulk orders of *The Simple Truth* for distribution are available at a discounted price. Please contact us for information and pricing.

Samya Johnson welcomes your questions and comments.
E-mail: info@calloflove.org

- Abraham's name occurs 69 times in the Quran. The Quran calls him the friend of Allah.

- The Quran claims Abraham wrote a holy book but that it was lost.

- Abraham believed in Allah and was a Muslim even before the dawn of Islam.

- Muslims claim to be the children of Abraham, through his son Ishmael.

in ISLAM

"Abraham was not a Jew nor yet a Christian but he was true in faith and bowed his will to Allah's..."

Quran 3:67

- Abraham is the greatest patriarch of the people of God. "He is the father of us all."

- Abraham was promised descendants as numerous as the stars in heaven.

- Abraham believed in the one true God whose name is Jehovah.

- Christians look to Abraham as an example of faith and obedience.

in CHRISTIANITY

"By faith Abraham, when called to go to a place he would later receive as his inheritance, obeyed and went."

Hebrews 11:8

Abrogation

in ISLAM

"When We [Allah] substitute one revelation for another, and Allah knows best what He reveals (in stages), they say, 'Thou art but a forger'..."

Quran 16:101

- Abrogation is an Islamic doctrine where verses revealed later in the Quran override earlier ones.

- Out of the 114 surahs (chapters) of the Quran, 71 are affected by this doctrine.

- Most abrogated verses emphasize violence and Jihad.[1]

- Muslims who embrace a peaceful Islam use abrogation conditionally.

in CHRISTIANITY

Jesus said: "Do not think that I came to abolish the Law or the Prophets; I did not come to abolish but to fulfill."

Matthew 5:17

- The Old Testament points to Christ through prophecies and promises.

- The New Testament records the fulfillment of those prophecies.

- Jesus came to fulfill the prophecies, not to abolish God's law.

- There is continuity in God's message from Genesis to Revelation.

---

[1] See "Jihad – Holy War" page 29, and "Jihad – Inner Strife" page 30.

- Adam was the first human created by Allah. He is regarded as a prophet.
- Angels were commanded to worship Adam.
- Adam was 90 feet tall. The height of man has been decreasing ever since.
- Allah taught Adam the names of all the creatures.

in ISLAM

"... thy Lord said to the angels: 'I am about to create man from clay: When I have... breathed into him of My spirit, fall ye down in obeisance unto him.'"

Quran 38:71-72

- God created the first man, Adam.
- Angels worship Christ, who is called the Last Adam, not the Adam of Genesis.
- Adam was made in the image of God. He had a close relationship with his Creator.
- God gave Adam the task of naming the animals in the garden.

in CHRISTIANITY

"Then the Lord God formed man of dust from the ground, and breathed into his nostrils the breath of life; and man became a living being."

Genesis 2:7

Adoption

in ISLAM

"...Nor has He [Allah] made your adopted sons your sons.... Call them by (the names of) their fathers, that is better in the sight of God."

Quran 33:4-5

- Muhammad did not have sons, so he adopted a male slave.

- Muhammad later abolished the "heresy of adoption" in order to marry his adopted son's wife.

- For this reason Muslims worldwide do not adopt.

- An orphan child cared for by a family is never legally theirs in name or inheritance.

in CHRISTIANITY

"He predestined us to adoption, as sons through Jesus Christ to Himself, according to the kind intention of His will."

Ephesians 1:5

- Earthly adoption is a reflection of the adoption believers experience with their Heavenly Father.

- Adoption into God's family is a permanent relationship.

- Christ-followers apply the biblical principle of adoption when they adopt an orphan.

- Adoption makes a child a member of the adopted family in every possible way.

- Muhammad prohibited Muslims from creating drawings or statues of people or animals.

- He taught that angels do not enter a house with pictures of creatures in it.

- Artists are limited to depict non-living things.

- Islamic art concentrates on calligraphy and geometric styles.

in ISLAM

"...Those who paint pictures would be punished on the Day of Resurrection and it would be said to them: breathe soul into what you have created."

Hadith Muslim, v. 24 # 5268

- God forbids creating images or statues for the purpose of worship.

- Having creative art that glorifies God does not keep God's presence out of the home.

- All Christians are encouraged to use their artistic gifts for the glory of God.

- Christian art spans a variety of styles and forms including statues and people.

in CHRISTIANITY

"God saw all that He had made, and behold, it was very good."

Genesis 1:31

The Bible

in ISLAM

"... Believe in Allah and His Messenger, and the scripture which He hath sent to His Messenger and the scripture which He sent to those before (him)..."

Quran 4:136

- Allah orders Muslims to accept the authority of the Pentateuch[2], the Psalms, and the Gospel[3].

- Isa (Jesus) came to confirm what Allah revealed through Moses.

- Muhammad encouraged his followers to consult "the people of the book"[4] when in doubt.

- Muslim leaders teach that arbitrary parts of the Bible have been changed.

in CHRISTIANITY

"But the word of the Lord endures forever. And this is the word which was preached to you."

I Peter 1:25

- Today's Bible is the same as it was in the 7th century, at the dawn of Islam.

- The Bible, inspired by God, is consistent and accurate.

- The almighty God protects His only message to humanity.

- History and archeology both document and confirm the consistency of the Bible.

---

[2] Genesis, Exodus, Leviticus, Numbers, and Deuteronomy.
[3] See "The Gospel" page 22.
[4] Christians and Jews.

in ISLAM

- Maryam (Mary) was Aaron's sister. She was an orphan fostered by Zachariah, father of John the Baptist.

- The angel told her she would bear a son as a virgin.

- She gave birth to Isa[5] in the desert under a palm tree.

- When Maryam brought the infant Isa to her town he spoke to defend his mother and to declare his prophethood.

"He [the angel] said 'Nay, I am only a messenger from thy Lord, (to announce) to thee the gift of a holy son.'"

Quran 19:19

in CHRISTIANITY

- Mary, Jesus' mother, who was a descendant of David, was engaged to Joseph.

- The angel Gabriel appeared to Mary telling her that the Holy Spirit would come upon her so that she would carry the Son of God.

- Jesus was born in Bethlehem, proclaimed by angels, and worshiped by shepherds and kings.

- As a child Jesus was raised by Mary and Joseph in Nazareth.

"She will bear a Son; and you shall call His name Jesus, for He will save His people from their sins."

Matthew 1:21

---

[5] Isa is the name the Quran uses to refer to Jesus.

Creation

in ISLAM

"Have not those who disbelieve known that.... We made every living thing of water?"

Quran 21:30

- The Quran states that Allah "made from water every living thing."

- In the Quran the number of creation days varies from four to eight to millions of years.

- There is no clear account of what was created each day.

- Allah expressed that he was not tired after he finished the creation.

in CHRISTIANITY

"By faith we understand that the universe was formed at God's command, so that what is seen was not made out of what was visible."

Hebrews 11:3

- God created the world from nothing.

- In Genesis, there are two accounts of the six-day creation.

- What was created in each of the six days is described in detail.

- God declared the seventh day a day of rest.

- The Quran teaches that Isa could not have died on the cross because he was sinless.

- Most Muslims believe Allah saved Isa from death by taking him to paradise.

- Other Muslims believe the crucifixion was a later story fabricated by Christians.

- By denying the crucifixion, Muslims believe they honor Isa.

in ISLAM

"...but they killed him not, nor crucified him, but so it was made to appear to them...Allah raised him up unto Himself ..."

Quran 4:157-158

- The Bible teaches that the sinless Jesus was crucified on the cross in place of sinners.

- Jesus chose to give His life. He rose again on the third day after His death.

- There is ample secular historical evidence for the crucifixion account.

- Without the crucifixion and the resurrection, Jesus would be like any other prophet.

in CHRISTIANITY

"...Christ died for our sins according to the Scriptures, and that He was buried, and that He was raised on the third day according to the Scriptures."

1 Corinthians 15:3-4

in ISLAM

"...When the call is proclaimed to prayer on Friday (the day of assembly), hasten earnestly to the remembrance of Allah..."

Quran 62:9

- Friday is the day of the week that Muslims observe as sacred.

- It is believed that the greatest verses in the Quran were given to Muhammad on Fridays.

- Islam claims that the final judgment will take place on a Friday.

- Congregational prayer is held in mosques at noon on Fridays. All Muslim men are expected to attend.

in CHRISTIANITY

"Now after He had risen early on the first day of the week, He first appeared to Mary Magdalene...."

Mark 16:9

- After creating the world God ordained the seventh day of the week as a day of rest.

- Jesus confirmed the need for a day of rest not as an oppressive legal practice but for the benefit of mankind.

- For Christians, Sunday became the day of worship and rest because Jesus rose from the dead on that day.

- Christians, both men and women, worship together on Sundays with prayer, praise, and fellowship.

- The declaration of faith, called the Shahadah, is the sign of conversion in Islam.

- The person must say it in Arabic for Allah to accept it.

- Anyone who confesses the Shahadah will be considered an infidel if they ever deny Islam.

- The Shahadah is repeated daily by Muslims during their conversations and prayers.

in ISLAM

"I confess that there is no god but Allah and I confess that Muhammad is the apostle of Allah."

Derived from Quran 3:18 and 63:1.

- A person embraces Christianity when they believe that Jesus is the Son of God.

- The Christian receives, by faith, God's gift of salvation through Jesus Christ.

- Christians declare their faith by confessing their sins and accepting Jesus as Lord.

- God continues to pursue and love those who choose to deny Christ.

in CHRISTIANITY

"If you confess with your mouth Jesus as Lord, and believe in your heart that God raised Him from the dead, you will be saved."

Romans 10:9

Divorce

in ISLAM

"So if a husband divorces his wife (irrevocably), he cannot, after that, remarry her until after she has married another husband and he has divorced her ..."

Quran 2:230

- The husband holds complete and uncontested power to divorce any of his wives for any reason.
- When he declares to his wife "I divorce you", the divorce becomes effective.
- The husband may grant his wife a divorce upon her request if he chooses.
- The husband holds exclusive custody of his children unless he chooses otherwise.

in CHRISTIANITY

Jesus said: "But I tell you that anyone who divorces his wife, except for sexual immorality, makes her the victim of adultery, and anyone who marries a divorced woman commits adultery."

Matthew 5:32

- God hates divorce.
- Divorce is permitted in the Bible only if there is infidelity.
- Divorce can be initiated by the husband or the wife.
- After divorce, both parents are encouraged to be involved in raising their children.

- Eve is not mentioned by name in the Quran. In Islamic tradition she is known as "Hawwa."

- The Quran mentions that a mate was created with Adam from the same soul.

- Muhammad claims that Eve was created from the most crooked portion of the rib, therefore she is fragile.

- Muhammad accuses Eve of betrayal; were it not for Eve, no woman would ever betray her husband.

in ISLAM

"O mankind, fear your Lord, who created you from one soul and created from it its mate and dispersed from both of them many men and women."

Quran 4:1

- Eve is a part of the creation account, along with Adam.

- Adam's loneliness moved God to quickly present him with a companion.

- God created Eve from Adam's rib. He created her in His own image, just like Adam.

- Both Adam and Eve are equally responsible for the fall of humanity.

in CHRISTIANITY

"Then the Lord God said, 'It is not good for the man to be alone; I will make him a helper suitable for him.'"

Genesis 2:18

Evil

in ISLAM

"And they (the disbelievers) schemed, and Allah schemed (against them): and Allah is the best of schemers."

Quran 3:54

- Allah is the supreme deceiver.
- He causes people to go astray with no explanation.
- He puts evil in whoever he chooses.
- Allah motivates people to sin.

in CHRISTIANITY

"God is not human, that He should lie, not a human being, that He should change His mind."

Numbers 23:19

- God does not lie or deceive. He is the Truth.
- God cannot be tempted by evil and He does not tempt anyone.
- God loves sinners, and longs for them to choose Him.
- God is all light. Darkness cannot exist in His presence.

Fasting - When and How

- Ramadan occurs once each lunar year. It lasts for 28 to 30 days.

- Muslims fast from sunrise to sunset. They celebrate and eat during the night.

- When fasting, Muslims refrain from food and drink.

- Muslims must avoid intimate relations, smoking, lying, and war while fasting.

in ISLAM

"Ramadan is the (month) in which was sent down the Qur'an, as a guide to mankind ..."

Quran 2:185

- A Christian can fast any time for a specific purpose when led by the Spirit to do so.

- The Bible gives various examples of how to fast.

- Jesus fasted for 40 days with no food or water.

- Daniel did a partial fast for 21 days, abstaining from all meat and sweets.

in CHRISTIANITY

Jesus said: "...when you fast, anoint your head and wash your face so that your fasting will not be noticed by men, but by your Father ..."

Matthew 6:17-18

Fasting - Why

in ISLAM

"O you who have believed, decreed upon you is fasting as it was decreed upon those before you that you may become righteous."

Quran 2:183

- Fasting is one of the five pillars of Islam.
- The primary fasting time for Muslims is during Ramadan.
- Fasting is commanded by Allah as a sign of submission to him.
- Muslims fast to be purified and to draw closer to Allah.

in CHRISTIANITY

"So I gave my attention to the Lord God to seek Him by prayer and supplications, with fasting, sackcloth and ashes."

Daniel 9:3

- Christians fast to humble themselves before God and grow closer to Him.
- Fasting is part of worship and spiritual growth.
- It helps Christ-followers focus on the spirit rather than the flesh.
- Jesus Christ takes away sins and makes believers righteous, not the act of fasting.

- Qadar (fate) is one of the six articles of faith in many Islamic sects. It is what Allah has already destined for every person.

- The choices a person makes are all previously determined by what they are destined to do.

- Most Muslims are driven by fate rather than self-initiated choices. The constant phrases they use are "if Allah wills" and "this is my fate."

- This belief is contradicted by another in the Quran which teaches that man can determine his own destiny by his works.

in ISLAM

"No misfortune can happen on earth or in your souls but is recorded in a decree before We bring it into existence..."

Quran 57:22

- Fate is not a biblical belief.
- The Bible teaches that people are responsible for their actions.
- Often, when the Bible speaks of destiny, it is referring to the choices a person makes.
- God presents people with the paths to life or death and longs for each person to choose life and obedience to Him.

in CHRISTIANITY

"'For I know the plans I have for you,' declares the Lord, 'plans to prosper you and not to harm you, plans to give you hope and a future.'"

Jeremiah 29:11

Father/Master

in ISLAM

"There is none in the heavens and the earth but cometh unto the Beneficent as a slave."

Quran 19:93

- In Islam's 99 names for Allah, none describe him as father.

- Allah is the master. He addresses Muslims in the Quran as slaves.

- Claiming that Allah has any human characteristics is unforgivable.

- Fatherhood can never be related to Allah. He does not need children. He is far above anything earthly.

in CHRISTIANITY

"Pray, then, in this way: 'Our Father who is in heaven, hallowed be Your name.'"

Matthew 6:9

- God is a personal God who calls Himself "Heavenly Father".

- The Bible refers to God as Father in both the Old and the New Testament.

- God expresses Himself through His Word with human characteristics so that people can know Him better.

- God calls believers His children, giving them the privilege to call Him "Abba Father".

- The complete biography of Muhammad is only told in secondary sources.

- Incidences of Muhammad's life are reported in much detail in the Hadith.

- The Quran confirms in several places that one must never disobey or lie to Muhammad.

- The Quran presents Muhammad as the perfect example of how to practice Islam.

in ISLAM

"And whatsoever the Messenger [Muhammad] giveth you, take it. And whatsoever he forbiddeth, abstain (from it)."

Quran 59:7

- Old Testament prophets foretell Jesus' life. The New Testament records His life on earth.

- The Bible records Jesus' message, teaching, and miracles. It does not tell particular details of His everyday life.

- Jesus is not just an example of belief, but the very source of belief and salvation.

- Jesus is not followed because He is a prophet, but because He is God Himself.

in CHRISTIANITY

"...This grace was given us in Christ Jesus before the beginning of time, but it has now been revealed through the appearing of our Savior, Christ Jesus, who has destroyed death and has brought life and immortality to light through the gospel."

2 Timothy 1:9b-10

in ISLAM

"And be steadfast in prayer; practice regular charity [Zakat]..."

Quran 2:43

- Zakat, or almsgiving, is one of the five pillars of Islam.
- Muslims believe it purifies their souls and increases their wealth.
- Zakat requires 2.5 to 5 percent to be given from surplus of annual income.
- Ramadan[6] is the best month to pay Zakat to gain more rewards from Allah.

in CHRISTIANITY

Jesus said: "Truly I tell you, this poor widow has put more into the treasury than all the others. They all gave out of their wealth; but she, out of her poverty, put in everything—all she had to live on."

Mark 12:43-44

- Tithing is giving at least 10 percent of one's total income.
- Giving reflects obedience and thanksgiving to the loving Father.
- Giving with pure motives is an expression of worship.
- Jesus taught that one should give in secret, and not seek recognition.

[6] See "Fasting – When and How" page 15

- Allah is the personal name of the god of Islam.

- Allah's singularity is his most important attribute.

- Allah is a progressive god. He replaces previous commands with contradictory new ones.

- Allah is the sovereign master who requires man to submit as an obedient slave.

in ISLAM

"Say: He is Allah, the One! Allah, the eternally besought of all! He begetteth not nor was begotten."

Quran 112:1-3

- "I Am" is the personal name of God, the Creator.

- The essence of God is an active personal love towards His creation.

- God is the same yesterday, today, and forever. Therefore His message does not change.

- God is the Heavenly Father who invites believers to call Him "Abba Father."

in CHRISTIANITY

"...The Lord is our God, the Lord is one."

Deuteronomy 6:4

The Gospel

in ISLAM

"...We bestowed on him [Isa] the Gospel wherein is guidance and light ..."

Quran 5:46

- The Quran teaches that the "Gospel" is the book Allah gave to Isa.
- For Muslims the gospel of Isa is not the same as the New Testament.
- The original gospel of Isa that points to Muhammad was corrupted by man.
- The four gospels of the Bible are not the true message of Isa.

in CHRISTIANITY

"For I would have you know, brethren, that the gospel which was preached by me is not according to man."

Galatians 1:11

- Jesus is the gospel, God's good news in the flesh.
- The New Testament contains the gospel message of Jesus Christ.
- The Old Testament scripture points towards Jesus and it has never changed.
- The true account of Jesus' life is found in the books of Matthew, Mark, Luke, and John.

- Hadith, in Arabic, means a narration or a report.

- The collection of Hadith is the sayings and actions of Muhammad, his wives, and his first followers.

- Hadith texts are used to interpret the Quran and to apply the detailed practices of Islam in all aspects of life.

- Most Muslims believe that the collection of Hadith is the second most esteemed resource after the Quran.

in ISLAM

"Ye have indeed in the messenger of Allah a beautiful pattern (of conduct) for any one whose hope is in Allah and the final day..."

Quran 33:21.

- The Bible is self-contained. It provides all knowledge necessary for salvation and holiness.

- Interpretations, commentaries, and applications of the Bible are not the Word of God.

- The Holy Spirit helps Christ-followers to understand the one true message of God.

- Denominational practices differ, but Bible-believing Christians share the mutual beliefs presented in the Word of God.

in CHRISTIANITY

Jesus said, "...You nullify the word of God by your tradition that you have handed down. And you do many things like that."

Mark 7:13

Halal and Haram

in ISLAM

"Forbidden to you (for food) are: dead meat, blood, the flesh of swine, and that on which hath been invoked the name of other than Allah."

Quran 5:3a

- Halal means allowed by Allah, or lawful.
- Haram means forbidden or prohibited by Allah.
- One main forbidden food is pork. Any pig-based product such as gelatin or lard is Haram.
- Devout Muslims follow this religious diet to minute details.

in CHRISTIANITY

"For everything God created is good, and nothing is to be rejected if it is received with thanksgiving."

I Timothy 4:4

- The New Testament advises Christians not to eat a food if it will make an unbeliever uncomfortable.
- In the Old Testament people were not to eat meat used for sacrifice.
- Every food created by God is good and should not be rejected.
- Jesus set an example by eating with His disciples, tax collectors, and other sinners.

- Janna is a materialistic and sensual paradise. It exists to satisfy the Muslim's physical desires.

- Delicious food, exquisite wines, beautiful huris[7], and servants are the source of pleasure in Janna.

- Women are separated from each other in Janna. Each lives in a separate "corner of a pearl," many miles away from the others.

- Allah's attribute of beauty will be seen by Muslims in Janna, but he will be unapproachable and unknowable.

in ISLAM

"As to the righteous, they will be in gardens... (To them will be said):"Eat and drink ye, with profit and health... and We shall join them to companions [Huris], with beautiful big and lustrous eyes."

Quran 52:17, 19, 20

- Heaven is the house of the Heavenly Father.

- Living eternally in the presence of God is the greatest joy for the Christian.

- People will all be like angels in heaven; there is no male or female.

- In heaven believers will worship Jesus in perfection and joy beyond understanding.

in CHRISTIANITY

"Beloved, now we are children of God, and it has not appeared as yet what we will be. We know that when He appears, we will be like Him, because we will see Him just as He is."

1 John 3:2

---

[7] Beautiful virgin creatures provided in paradise for Muslim men to enjoy.

Hell

in ISLAM

"Verily, Allah has cursed the unbelievers and prepared for them a blazing fire, to dwell therein forever."

Quran 33:64-65b

- There is no description of hell in the Quran, except that it is full of fire and smoke.

- Dwellers of hell sigh, wail, and are wretched.

- The Quran teaches that every Muslim must pass through hell before they enter Janna.[8]

- The Hadith teaches that after death every Muslim walks on a very thin rope that hangs over hell. Some will fall as they pass, and others will cross over to paradise.

in CHRISTIANITY

"...Those who do not obey the gospel of our Lord Jesus...will pay the penalty of eternal destruction, away from the presence of the Lord and from the glory of His power."

2 Thessalonians 1:8-9

- Hell is the eternal destiny for those who reject Christ.

- The Bible describes hell with terms like brimstone, fire, weeping, and gnashing of teeth.

- Hell is a place where God is absent; therefore the intense anguish involves mental, physical, and spiritual distress.

- After death, Christ-followers immediately enter the presence of their loving God.

[8] See "Heaven" page 25.

in ISLAM

- Muhammad claimed that Allah took him to Jerusalem, the "farthest mosque," on the back of a winged mule.

- This event is known as "the Night Journey" and is recorded in one verse in the Quran.

- Hadith expands on the Quranic verse to say that Muhammad was escorted through heaven and greeted by prophets.

- Islam's declaration of ownership to the 'farthest mosque', called the 'Al-Aqsa mosque', and by proxy the city of Jerusalem, is based solely on this one verse and its interpretations.

"Glory to (Allah) who did take His Servant for a journey by night from the Sacred Mosque to the Farthest Mosque... in order that We might show him some of Our signs."

Quran 17:1

in CHRISTIANITY

- A biblical doctrine is formed from the entire Bible, not from one verse pulled out of context.

- Jesus' earthly ministry included many recorded visits to Jerusalem.

- Jerusalem plays a major role in both the Old and New Testaments as a center of key events.

- The Bible contains many prophesies about the City of Jerusalem.

"Pray for the peace of Jerusalem; May those who love you be secure."

Psalm 122:6

Jesus

in ISLAM

"He [Isa] was no more than a servant: We granted our favor to him, and We made him an example to the children of Israel."

Quran 43:59

- The Quran claims that Isa[9] was a mere human being, sent as a prophet to confirm the message before him.

- Isa is not the son of Allah. Islam considers it blasphemy to say so.

- Isa healed the sick and breathed life into clay birds.

- Isa was not crucified; instead, he was rescued by Allah and taken to paradise.

in CHRISTIANITY

"Jesus said to her, 'I am the resurrection and the life; he who believes in me will live even if he dies.'"

John 11:25

- Jesus has existed since the beginning of time. He became man as foretold in the Old Testament.

- Jesus is the Son of God, not in the human sense, but by a divine and eternal relationship with His Father.

- Jesus healed the sick, raised the dead, and performed many other miracles.

- Jesus died on the cross to pay the price for sin. He conquered death and rose again.

---

[9] Isa is the name the Quran uses to refer to Jesus

Jihad - Holy War

in ISLAM

- Jihad or holy war is not an option for Muslims, it is mandated by Allah.
- Jihad is fighting for the cause of Allah to protect and expand Islam.
- The target of holy Jihad is every non-Muslim.
- All of the Medinan[10] verses in the Quran about Jihad refer to Jihad as a duty of holy war.

"Fighting [Jihad] is prescribed for you, and ye dislike it. But it is possible that ye dislike a thing which is good for you ..."

Quran 2:216

in CHRISTIANITY

- The Bible does not teach that war is a means to spread the message of God.
- In the Old Testament war was a grim necessity for God to punish national sins.
- War was never a tool to glorify a person or a nation for material gain.
- Jesus teaches His followers to love their enemies and to pray for those who persecute them.

"Never take your own revenge, beloved, but leave room for the wrath of God, for it is written, 'Vengeance is Mine, I will repay,' says the Lord."

Romans 12:19

---

[10] Verses given to Muhammad during the later part of his life in the city of Medina, Saudi Arabia.

Jihad - Inner Strife

in ISLAM

"And strive for Allah with the endeavor which is His right.... So establish worship, pay the poor-due, and hold fast to Allah..."

Quran 22:78

- Jihad is Arabic for "utmost effort" or "strife."
- Jihad holds a wide range of meanings, from the Muslim experiencing spiritual and physical strife, to believers actively fighting for the cause of Islam.
- In its peaceful form, Jihad is the Muslim's physical and mental sacrifice to please Allah.
- Praying, fasting, pilgrimage, and reading the Quran are all examples of peaceful Jihad.

in CHRISTIANITY

"Now those who belong to Christ Jesus have crucified the flesh with its passions and desires. If we live by the Spirit, let us also walk by the Spirit."

Galatians 5:24-25

- Christians strive to be more Christ-like. This is called sanctification.
- Sanctification can only be accomplished by yielding to the transforming power of the Holy Spirit.
- Spiritual perseverance is part of being transformed.
- The Bible teaches that Christ-followers are being perfected; they are not perfect.

- Allah determined Arabic to be the language of Islam.

- A Muslim must perform the five daily prayers in Arabic to be accepted by Allah.

- The Quran is written in ancient Arabic, and Muslims believe that its meaning transcends translation.

- After death every Muslim must answer the angel's questions in Arabic as a test.

in ISLAM

"[It is] an Arabic Qur'an, without any deviance that they might become righteous."

Quran 39:28

- Throughout the Bible God spoke to people in their own languages.

- Christianity can be practiced in every language by all people.

- The books of the Bible were written in Hebrew, Aramaic, and Greek over the course of 1,600 years and are still true when translated.

- God created all languages and He accepts worship in all languages.

in CHRISTIANITY

"If I speak in the tongues of men or of angels, but do not have love, I am only a resounding gong or a clanging cymbal."

1 Corinthians 13:1

Lying

in ISLAM

"Allah will not call you to account for thoughtlessness in your oaths, but for the intention in your hearts..."

Quran 2:225

- Allah does not judge the Muslims' words but what they determine in their hearts.

- The Quran states that lying is acceptable. It even teaches how to make amends for breaking an oath.

- Muslims are allowed to deny their faith for self-preservation.

- Muhammad allowed lying in three situations: war, to reconcile two parties, and to avoid marital conflict.

in CHRISTIANITY

Jesus said: "But let your statement be, 'Yes, yes' or 'No, no'; anything beyond these is of evil."

Matthew 5:37

- The Bible teaches that lying is a sin in all circumstances.

- Sins are not judged on different levels, liars and murderers are in the same category.

- Jesus teaches that denying Him will result in separation from God.

- Lying is a tool of Satan who is called "the father of lies."

- Polygamy is a normal practice in Islam. Wives can be exchanged one for another.

- Marriage is a contract of ownership between the husband and the bride's guardian.

- A dowry is the price paid by the bridegroom to possess his bride.

- Marriage is a duty to be fulfilled by every Muslim to expand the Umma[11] of Islam.

in ISLAM

"Fair in the eyes of men is the love of things they covet: Women and sons...horses ... and well-tilled land ..."

Quran 3:14

- Marriage is between one man and one woman.

- It is a sacred covenant in front of God, not a financial transaction.

- Love, unity, and sacrificial giving from both spouses are the basis of marriage.

- Marriage is honored in the Bible, but not commanded of everyone. A single person is of equal value in God's eyes.

in CHRISTIANITY

"Marriage should be honored by all, and the marriage bed kept pure, for God will judge the adulterer and all the sexually immoral."

Hebrews 13:4

---

[11] The population of Islam's followers.

Marriage - Polygamy

in ISLAM

"... Marry women of your choice, two or three or four; but if ye fear that ye shall not be able to deal justly (with them), then only one..."

Quran 4:3

- A Muslim man can marry up to four women at the same time.

- The Quran allows men to take concubines from among captives and slaves.

- Muslim men are allowed temporary marriages to fulfill their needs when traveling.

- Allah gave Muhammad special privileges to have as many women as he desired.

in CHRISTIANITY

"[Jesus] said, 'Have you not read that He who created them from the beginning made them male and female, and said, for this reason a man shall leave his father and mother and be joined to his wife, and the two shall become one flesh?'"

Matthew 19:4-5

- Jesus Christ confirmed what God established in Genesis: marriage is between one man and one woman.

- Polygamy in the Bible is a result of rebellion against God's plan.

- In marriage, the husband and wife become one flesh. Pursuing or forming additional relationships is adultery.

- God does not give special privileges to prophets or leaders concerning marriage or any other matter.

- A wife must be managed by her husband because she is a weak creature.

- She is referred to as a possession such as gold, silver, cattle, and land.

- A woman is considered to be at the mercy of her husband's physical and sexual needs.

- A man is to discipline and beat his wives when they do not please him.

in ISLAM

"As for those [women] from whom ye fear rebellion, admonish them and banish them to beds apart, and scourge [beat] them."

Quran 4:34

- A husband is to love his wife as much as Jesus loved the Church, and died for her.

- A husband is to love his wife as he loves his own body.

- He is not to be angry or harsh with her.

- A wife is a partner with her husband.

in CHRISTIANITY

"Husbands, love your wives, just as Christ also loved the church and gave Himself up for her."

Ephesians 5:25

Martyrdom

in ISLAM

"... To him who fighteth in the cause of Allah, whether he is slain or gets victory, soon shall We give him a reward of great (value)."

Quran 4:74

- Martyrdom is a tool to expand and protect the religion of Islam.
- Dying for the cause of Islam guarantees an afterlife in paradise.
- Martyrs buy their direct path to paradise. They avoid passing through hell and judgment.
- Securing eternal delight through martyrdom is a choice any Muslim can make.

in CHRISTIANITY

"For Christ's love compels us... He died for all, that those who live should no longer live for themselves but for Him who died for them and was raised again."

2 Corinthians 5:14-15

- Jesus the Son of God willingly laid down His life and paid the price for sin.
- Biblical martyrdom is about never denying your faith, even if it costs you your life.
- Christ shed His blood to give His followers assurance of eternal life with Him.
- Christians have no need to earn salvation through martyrdom.

- Miracles are the confirmation of a prophet's authenticity.
- The Quran confirms that Moses and Isa performed miracles.
- The Quran states very clearly that Muhammad did not perform miracles.
- The one miracle attributed to Muhammad by Islam is Allah giving him the Quran.

in ISLAM

"Or they say: He hath invented it [the Quran]. Say: Then bring ten surahs,[12] the like thereof, invented, and call on everyone ye can beside Allah, if ye are truthful!"

Quran 11:13

- God uses miracles to confirm His hand upon His prophets.
- God uses miracles to show His might or draw people closer to Him.
- The miracles that Jesus performed bear witness that God the Father sent Him.
- Jesus healed the sick, fed the hungry, raised the dead, made the lame walk and the blind see.

in CHRISTIANITY

"The people were amazed when they saw the mute speaking, the crippled made well, the lame walking and the blind seeing. And they praised the God of Israel."

Matthew 15:31

[12] Chapters of the Quran.

in ISLAM

"The Prophet said, 'when any human being is born, Satan touches him at both sides of the body with his two fingers...'"

Hadith Bukhari, v. 4 # 506

- "Original sin" in the Quran refers only to the first mistake committed by Adam.
- Adam's mistake affected only him. It does not affect his descendants.
- Humans are born sinless and neutral, and then Satan touches them.
- Sin is an outward action not a heart issue. It can be paid for by good works and through Allah's mercy.

in CHRISTIANITY

"For the wages of sin is death, but the free gift of God is eternal life in Christ Jesus our Lord."

Romans 6:23

- Sin first entered the world through the disobedience of Adam and Eve.
- All mankind inherited the sinful nature of Adam.
- Humans are born in sin and Satan uses this against them.
- Sin is an offense against God, therefore its price is death.

- Pilgrimage (Hajj) is one of the five pillars of Islam that must be completed by every Muslim, with few exceptions. Hajj purifies the Muslim.

- Muslims make pilgrimage to Mecca and other holy sites in Saudi Arabia.

- Hajj takes place in the 12th month of the Muslim lunar calendar.

- Preparing for the Hajj and participating in it take a total of 10 to 14 days.

in ISLAM

"And pilgrimage to the House is a duty unto God for mankind, for him who can find the way thither."

Quran 3:97

- The Bible teaches that life is a pilgrimage, a journey towards heaven.

- Some Christians visit the Holy Land to connect with the places Jesus walked on earth.

- Visiting the places Christ walked does not cleanse from sins.

- Every Christ-follower is a pilgrim, saved by grace, doing God's work on earth.

in CHRISTIANITY

Jesus said: "...you will worship the Father neither on this mountain nor in Jerusalem...Yet a time is coming and has now come when the true worshipers will worship the Father in the Spirit and in truth."

John 4:21-23

Prayer - How Often

in ISLAM

" 'I ask you by Allah. Has Allah ordered you to offer five prayers in a day and night (24 hours)...?' He [Muhammad] replied, 'By Allah, Yes.'"

Hadith Bukhari, v. 1, # 63

- The required five daily prayers is one of the five pillars of Islam. It is never mentioned in the Quran, only in the Hadith.

- Muhammad bargained with Allah through Moses to reduce the required daily prayers from fifty to five.

- Muhammad claimed that Gabriel taught him when and how to perform the five prayers.

- The Muslim is promised greater rewards in exchange for any additional prayers they perform.

in CHRISTIANITY

"Rejoice always; pray without ceasing; in everything give thanks; for this is God's will for you in Christ Jesus."

I Thessalonians 5:16-18

- The Bible teaches that prayer is a natural part of the Christian's life.

- Throughout His life on earth, Jesus gave many examples of how and when to pray.

- The Lord's Prayer is an example of what prayers should include when Christians talk to their Heavenly Father.

- The Word of God teaches to pray without ceasing.

- Proper ritual performance is of utmost importance for Allah to accept a prayer as worthy.

- Cleanliness of the body is stressed more than the connection with Allah.

- Prayers are assigned phrases from the Quran that should be repeated.

- Prayers must be said in correctly pronounced Arabic regardless of the Muslim's language of origin.

in ISLAM

"...When ye rise up for prayer, wash you faces, and your hands up to the elbows, and lightly rub your heads and (wash) your feet up to the ankles..."

Quran 5:6

- Prayer is not tied to specific times or words.

- It is a two-way conversation between God and the Christian.

- Christians pray with the guidance of the Holy Spirit, in the name of Jesus Christ.

- Prayer is not bound to a specific language, place, or format.

in CHRISTIANITY

Jesus said: "And when you pray, do not be like the hypocrites, for they love to pray standing in the synagogues and on the street corners to be seen by others."

Matthew 6:5

Prayer - Purpose

in ISLAM

"Be guardians of your prayers, and of the midmost prayer, and stand up with devotion to Allah..."

Quran 2:238

- Prayer is required of every Muslim.
- It is an expression of submission to Allah, but does not allow the Muslim to have a relationship with him.
- Prayer is considered a good deed.
- It acts as a token to erase some of the Muslims' bad deeds.

in CHRISTIANITY

"Be anxious for nothing, but in everything by prayer and supplication with thanksgiving let your requests be made known to God."

Philippians 4:6

- Prayer is an important part of the Christian's intimate relationship with the Heavenly Father.
- Christians pray to worship God, magnify, and glorify Him.
- Through prayer Christians can cast their cares before the Lord.
- Prayer is one way to listen to God speak.

- The Quran teaches that prophets are men chosen by Allah and given a message to deliver to a specific people group.

- Countless prophets came before Muhammad.

- Every prophet called his people to worship Allah and follow Islam, including Abraham, Moses, and Isa.

- The final and greatest prophet that Allah sent was Muhammad.

in ISLAM

"Muhammad is not the father of any of your men, but (he is) the Messenger of Allah, and the seal of the prophets..."

Quran 33:40

- The Bible teaches that God calls prophets to deliver a message for a specific purpose.

- True prophecy always originates from God Himself.

- Prophets told of future events that have and will come true.

- Prophets pointed to Jesus, the coming Messiah. They did not glorify themselves.

in CHRISTIANITY

"In the past God spoke to our ancestors through the prophets... but in these last days He has spoken to us by His Son, whom He appointed heir of all things, and through whom also He made the universe."

Hebrews 1:1-2

Salvation

in ISLAM

"And decidedly not one of you ...except that he will go (herded) down to it [hell]; that, for your Lord, has been a thing decreed a must..."

Quran 19:71

- "Rewards," not "salvation," is the word used in the Quran to describe eternal bliss.

- Muslims who perform good deeds will be rewarded with paradise. The wicked will be punished in hell.

- The good and evil deeds of a Muslim will be weighed on a scale.

- Muhammad informed Muslims that their eternal destiny is not guaranteed. All must pass through hell first.

in CHRISTIANITY

"For by grace you have been saved through faith; and that not of yourselves, it is the gift of God; not as a result of works, so that no one may boast."

Ephesians 2:8-9

- Salvation from eternal death is God's good news.

- Salvation depends entirely on the work of Jesus on the cross, not on good works.

- Good works are a natural expression of the Christian's faith.

- Jesus promised that whoever believes in Him will not perish but will have eternal life with Him.

- Satan was one of the Jinn.[13] He was the best among them and elevated to a high position.

- Allah cursed Satan when he did not bow down before Adam.

- The Quran talks about Iblis (Satan) as a physical being created from fire.

- He is a rebellious creature who touches every human at birth so that they will commit evil acts.

in ISLAM

"...Satan is an enemy to you.... He only invites his adherents that they may become companions of the blazing fire."

Quran 35:6

- Lucifer was a chief angel with special beauty and power.

- Lucifer, Satan, and the devil are all names for the same fallen angel.

- He wanted to rise above God, so he was cast out of heaven with the angels who followed him.

- Satan is the ruler of this world, who works to control people's hearts. He will be eternally punished for this on Judgment Day.

in CHRISTIANITY

"...be on the alert. Your adversary, the devil, prowls around like a roaring lion, seeking someone to devour."

I Peter 5:8

[13] See "Spiritual Beings" page 52.

Second Coming

in ISLAM

"And he (Isa) shall be a sign (for the coming of) the hour (of judgment): therefore have no doubt about the (hour)..."

Quran 43:61

- Muslims believe that Isa will return to judge the world.
- According to the Hadith Isa will come as a Muslim ruler. He will "break the crosses" and "kill the pigs."
- Isa will convert Christians and Jews to Islam.
- He will live on earth for 40 years. Then he will die and be buried in Medina next to Muhammad.

in CHRISTIANITY

"This Jesus, who has been taken up from you into heaven, will come in just the same way as you have watched Him go into heaven."

Acts 1:11

- Jesus will return to judge the living and the dead.
- People from all languages, races, and religions will bow down before Jesus.
- Jesus will judge all who did not believe in Him throughout the ages.
- Jesus will never see death again but will reign forever.

- The Islamic judiciary system practiced in most Muslim countries is called "Sharia Law."

- Sharia is derived from the Quran and the Hadith.

- Religious and community life are dictated by Sharia Law.

- Some of the harsh Sharia laws include amputation of hands for stealing, eighty lashes for drinking, and stoning to death for adultery.

in ISLAM

"Verily, this is My way, leading straight: follow it: follow not (other) paths: they will scatter you about from His (great) path: thus doth He command you. that ye may be righteous."

Quran 6:153

- The law of the Lord is written in the Christian's heart.

- The law in the Bible is God's commandments to His people.

- The Christian follows the law of God out of love, not fear.

- Jesus commands His followers to submit to the civil laws of their country.

THE LAW of THE LORD

"I desire to do your will, my God; your law is within my heart."

Psalm 40:8

Sin

in ISLAM

"Whom Allah doth guide, he is on the right path: whom He rejects from His guidance such are the persons who perish"

Quran 7:178

- Sin is regarded as a mistake that can be corrected rather than a permanent offense against Allah.

- Allah breathed wickedness into humans causing their natural tendency for evil.

- No one is free to choose good or evil. Allah decides for them at birth.

- Sins are not equal. Allah forgives small sins and punishes big sins.

in CHRISTIANITY

"Let no one say when he is tempted, 'I am being tempted by God'; for God cannot be tempted by evil, and He Himself does not tempt anyone."

James 1:13

- Sin is defined clearly in the Bible as rebellion against God.

- Sin never originates from God, but from Satan and human sinful nature.

- Man has to choose between good and evil. God's love compels believers towards good.

- All sins deserve equal punishment. Through faith in Christ all sin is forgiven.

- The relationship of the Muslim to Allah is that of a slave to an owner.

- The approval of Allah is based entirely on the actions of the Muslim.

- Allah's love is conditional and dependent on the Muslim's performance.

- Allah does not love the whole world.

in ISLAM

"For Allah loveth those who do good."

Quran 5:93

- The relationship of the Christ-follower to God is that of a child to their father.

- God loves every person even if they don't love Him.

- God pours His love and blessings on the evil and the good.

- God initiates love.

in CHRISTIANITY

"He tends His flock like a shepherd: He gathers the lambs in His arms and carries them close to His heart; He gently leads those that have young."

Isaiah 40:11

Son of God

in ISLAM

"It is not befitting to (the majesty of) Allah that He should beget a son."

Quran 19:35

- The Quran uses the term "Son of God" in the physical sense.
- Islam considers the phrase "Son of God" blasphemy.
- It assumes "Son of God" means that Isa was born as a result of a physical relationship between God and Mary.
- Isa was an ordinary man but later Christians made him the Son of God.

in CHRISTIANITY

"For to us a child is born, to us a son is given, and the government will be on His shoulders. And He will be called Wonderful Counselor, Mighty God, Everlasting Father, Prince of Peace."

Isaiah 9:6

- The word "son" is the best way humans can understand the intimate relationship between God the Father and Jesus Christ.
- The Father-Son relationship between God the Father and Jesus is not through creation or procreation.
- In the beginning Jesus was with God and He was God.
- The Bible confirms the unique relationship between God the Father and His Son Jesus Christ.

- Muslims claim that Abraham offered Ishmael and not Isaac as a sacrifice, although the Quran never mentions the child's name.

- The greatest feast of Islam is Eid al-Adha, the sacrifice feast, commemorating Abraham's willingness to sacrifice Ishmael to Allah.

- Abraham and Ishmael traveled together to Mecca and built the Ka'aba. Ishmael is considered the ancestor of Arabs including Muhammad.

- The Quran teaches that Isaac is Abraham's second son and a prophet.

in ISLAM

"Then, when (the son) reached (the age of) (serious) work with him [Abraham], he said: 'O my son! I see in vision that I offer thee in sacrifice'..."

Quran 37:102

- God asked Abraham to sacrifice his beloved son Isaac as an offering.

- God promised to bless Ishmael, Abraham's son from Hagar, with a great nation.

- Ishmael lived apart from Abraham. His descendants became the Ishmaelites.

- Abraham's willingness to sacrifice Isaac foreshadows God's willingness to sacrifice His own beloved Son on the cross.

in CHRISTIANITY

"By faith Abraham, when he was tested, offered up Isaac, and he who had received the promises was offering up his only begotten son."

Hebrews 11:17

Spiritual Beings

in ISLAM

"Behold! We said to the angels, 'bow down to Adam': They bowed down except Iblis. He was one of the Jinns, and he broke the command of his Lord..."

Quran 18:50

- Jinns are powerful intelligent beings who can be seen by humans.

- Jinns are created from fire. Some are good and others are evil.

- Angels have no gender and are made of light.

- Angels are messengers who are completely obedient to Allah.

in CHRISTIANITY

"For by Him all things were created, both in the heavens and on earth, visible and invisible, whether thrones or dominions or rulers or authorities—all things have been created through Him and for Him."

Colossians 1:16

- Angels can be messengers of God.

- God uses angels to protect and rescue His children.

- Angels surround the throne of God, continuously serving and worshiping Him.

- Satan and his minions are fallen angels who rebelled against God.

- Allah gave Moses laws on a stone tablet that he took to his people.

- Angered by their idol worship, Moses set the tablets aside and later picked them up.

- In three places in the Quran there are commentaries on the laws Allah gave to Moses.

- The ten commandments in the Quran do not match the Ten Commandments of the Bible.

in ISLAM

"And We ordained laws for him [Moses] in the tablets in all matters, both commanding and explaining all things..."

Quran 7:145

- God gave Moses the Ten Commandments, which he then took to the people of Israel.

- Angered by their idol worship, Moses broke the tablets.

- In another encounter with God he was given the Ten Commandments again.

- The Ten Commandments are the foundation on which Christians build obedient lives to God.

in CHRISTIANITY

"Therefore no one will be declared righteous in God's sight by the works of the law; rather, through the law we become conscious of our sin."

Romans 3:20

Trinity

in ISLAM

"So believe in Allah and His messengers. Say not 'Trinity': desist: it will be better for you: for Allah is one Allah."

Quran 4:171

- Islam believes that Allah is numerically one.

- The Quran claims that Christians believe in three individual gods: God, Mary, and Jesus.

- Muslims are encouraged to correct and admonish those who believe in three gods.

- Muslims reject the concept of the trinity and consider it blasphemy.

in CHRISTIANITY

"Go therefore and make disciples of all the nations, baptizing them in the name of the Father and the Son and the Holy Spirit."

Matthew 28:19

- The Lord God is one in essence.

- The triune God of the Bible is the Father, the Son, and the Holy Spirit.

- The Bible teaches that God is three persons in one, simultaneously and continuously.

- The perfect love and unity of the triune God is a model of the oneness and love that characterizes the Christian faith.

The Veil

- The veil, or hijab, literally means a concealer that makes a thing invisible.

- A woman's body is full of temptation. She must keep it totally covered to avoid being molested.

- Women who wear the hijab are usually more devout Muslims. They believe they have a better chance of going to paradise.

- Wearing the hijab is a sign of submission to Allah, to the husband, and any male guardian.

in ISLAM

"O Prophet! Tell thy wives and daughters, and the believing women, that they should cast their outer garments over their persons...that they should be known (as such) and not molested..."

Quran 33:59

- The Bible instructs women to dress modestly and avoid extravagance.

- There is nothing inherently wrong with the female body. She is created in God's image.

- Nothing a woman wears assures her entrance to heaven.

- A woman who is a true Christ-follower will naturally reflect this in her attire and appearance.

in CHRISTIANITY

"Now the Lord is the Spirit, and where the Spirit of the Lord is, there is liberty."

2 Corinthians 3:17

Women - Equality

in ISLAM

"Men are in charge of women, because Allah hath made the one of them to excel the other, and because they spend of their property (for the support of women)..."

Quran 4:34

- Men are superior to women because Allah ordained it so.

- Women's limitations are caused by their weak mental abilities.

- Women cannot understand religion in the same way men do because they are ungrateful by nature.

- Every Muslim woman must always have a male guardian at all stages of life: father, brother, husband, or son.

in CHRISTIANITY

"God created man in His own image, in the image of God He created him; male and female He created them."

Genesis 1:27

- Men and women are equal in the eyes of God because they are both created in His image.

- A woman's personal relationship with God is not related to her gender.

- Women can serve God with equal mental abilities to men.

- God shows no favoritism. He expects both men and women to respond to His message in the same way.

- The majority of Muslim women are destined for hell.

- Obedience to her husband and raising her children in the Muslim way offers a woman a better chance of rescue from hell.

- The key expression of a Muslim woman's faith is total submission to her husband.

- Men are promised many pleasures in paradise, including beautiful women and Huris.[14] Women have no specific promises in paradise.

in ISLAM

"Muhammad said: 'I was shown the hell-fire and that the majority of its dwellers were women who were ungrateful.'"

Hadith Bukhari, v. 1 # 28

- Everyone, male or female, who believes in Jesus, will have eternal life.

- Salvation is given by God to both men and women through His grace.

- A Christian woman submits to her husband out of love, not fear.

- Women are equal heirs in the kingdom of God.

in CHRISTIANITY

"...There is neither slave nor free man, there is neither male nor female; for you are all one in Christ Jesus."

Galatians 3:28

---

14 Huris are beautiful virgin creatures provided in paradise for Muslim men to enjoy.

Women - Witness

in ISLAM

"...Get two witnesses, out of your own men, and if there are not two men, then a man and two women... so that if one of them errs, the other can remind her..."

Quran 2:282

- A woman's trustworthiness is not equal to a man's.
- Inability to be intelligent or reliable is the main reason a woman is not an equal witness.
- A woman's share in inheritance is half of her brother.
- She can never be an independent complete person because her character is by nature defective.

in CHRISTIANITY

"Now if we are children, then we are heirs; heirs of God and co-heirs with Christ, if indeed we share in His sufferings in order that we may also share in His glory."

Romans 8:17

- Jesus entrusted a woman, Mary Magdalene, to tell the disciples that He had risen.
- Jesus regards women as equal in all aspects.
- Christian parents are to provide justly and impartially for their daughters and sons.
- A Christian woman is a complete person in the sight of God regardless of the presence of men in her life.

- Other than believing in Allah, Muhammad, and the Quran, faith in Islam is defined by works.

- Works include but are not limited to fasting, praying, pilgrimage, and giving.

- Works determine who the person is in Allah's eyes.

- Works are the gateway to pleasing Allah and gaining his favor.

in ISLAM

"And spend of your substance [wealth] in the cause of Allah... for Allah loveth those who do good."

Quran 2:195

- Works are the natural expression of the Christian's faith.

- "Love your neighbor as you love yourself" is the principle behind how true Christ-followers live their faith.

- Faith and not works defines who a Christian is before God.

- A person can never earn salvation through works.

in CHRISTIANITY

"For by grace you have been saved through faith; and that not of yourselves, it is the gift of God; not as a result of works, so that no one may boast."

Ephesians 2:8-9

The Written Revelation

in ISLAM

"And unto thee have We revealed the scripture with the truth, confirming whatever scripture was before it, and a watcher over it."

Quran 5:48

- Muslims claim that the Quran is the final revelation sent by Allah to humanity.

- The Quran is the collection of what Allah revealed to Muhammad over a period of 20 years. It was compiled in 650 AD, 18 years after his death.

- Muslims claim that the Quran cannot be matched grammatically or linguistically by any human.

- The Quran is divided into 114 chapters (suras) organized by length, not by chronological order.

in CHRISTIANITY

"For the word of God is living and active and sharper than any two-edged sword and piercing as far as the division of soul and spirit..."

Hebrews 4:12

- The Bible is God's only written revelation to humanity.

- The Holy Spirit inspired more than 40 different authors over the course of almost 1,600 years.

- The 66 books of the Old and the New Testaments present the unified continuous message of God to humanity.

- The message of the Bible is current and universal.

REFERENCES

Hadith search website: www.alim.org/library/hadith/SHB/I/I
Quran search website: www.quran.com
Bible website: www.biblegateway.com

Abraham

In Islam:
- Quran 4:125
- Quran 87:19, 4:163
- Quran 3:67, 22:78
- Quran 2:127-128

In Christianity:
- Romans 4:16
- Genesis 12:1-3
- Romans 4:17
- Hebrews 11:8-9

Abrogation

In Islam:
- Quran 16:101
- www.answering-islam.org/Silas/ abrogation.htm (Examples: Quran 9:29 abrogates Quran 2:109)
- Quran 2:256 is replaced or abrogated by Quran 9:5, 47:5, 9:29, 8:39, 9:3
- www.meforum.org/1754/peace-or-jihad-abrogation-in-islam

In Christianity:
- Isaiah 53
- Jeremiah 31:31-34
- Matthew 5:17
- II Timothy 3:16-17

Adam

In Islam:
- Quran 38:71-72
- Quran 2:34
- Hadith Bukhari 4:543
- Quran 2:31

In Christianity:
- Genesis 2:7
- Revelation 5:11
- Genesis 1:27
- Genesis 2:19

Adoption

In Islam:
- Quran 33:37-40, Hadith Bukhari 9:516
- Quran 33:4
- Hadith Bukhari 7:25, 6:305
- Quran 33:5

In Christianity:
- Ephesians 1:5
- John 1:12
- James 1:27, Matthew 18:5
- Romans 8:14-16

Art

In Islam:
- Hadith Bukhari 3:428
- Hadith Bukhari 4:448
- Hadith Bukhari 9:646
- www.metmuseum.org/toah/hd/ geom/hd_geom.htm

In Christianity:
- Exodus 20:23
- Genesis 1:31
- Matthew 25:14-30
- I Corinthians 10:31

The Bible

In Islam:
- Quran 5:46, 3:184
- Quran 3:3, 4:136
- Quran 10:94
- Quran 2:59

In Christianity:
- II Peter 1:20-21
- II Timothy 3:16
- Revelation 22:18
- www.answering-islam.org/Bible/ index.html

The Christmas Story

In Islam:
- Quran 3:37
- Quran 19:16-21
- Quran 19:23
- Quran 19:30-33

In Christianity:
- Luke 3:23-38
- Luke 1:28-32
- Luke 2:1-21, Micah 5:2
- Luke 2:39-40

Creation

In Islam:
- Quran 21:30
- Quran 7:54, 70:4, 22:47, 41:19-12
- Quran 79:27-33
- Quran 50:38

In Christianity:
- Genesis 1:1, Hebrews 11:3
- Genesis 1 and 2
- Genesis 1 and 2
- Genesis 2:2

The Cross

In Islam:
- Quran 4:157
- Quran 4:158
- www.answering-islam.org/ authors/adams/crucifixion_ confusion.html
- Quran 3:55

In Christianity:
- Hebrews 7:26, 1 Peter 2:22, I Corinthians 15:3-4
- John 10:17-18
- www.knowwhatyoubelieve.com
- I Corinthians 15:17-19

Day of Worship

In Islam:
- Quran 62:9
- Hadith Abu-Dawood 400
- Hadith Muslim 417
- Quran 62:9

In Christianity:
- Genesis 2:2-3
- Mark 2:27
- Mark 16:9
- John 20:19, Acts 20:7

Declaration of Faith

In Islam:
- Quran 3:18, 63:1
- Quran 12:2
- Quran 2:39, Hadith Bukhari 9:37
- www.answering-islam.org/Index/S/shahada.html

In Christianity:
- Romans 10:9-10
- Ephesians 2:8-9
- John 1:12-13, Romans 10:9-10
- John 3:16

Divorce

In Islam:
- Quran 4:34-35
- Hadith Muslim 706
- Quran 65:1-2, 2:229
- www.expertlaw.com/library/family_law/islamic_custody-3.html#80

In Christianity:
- Malachi 2:16
- Matthew 5:32
- I Corinthians 7:15
- Proverbs 22:6

Eve

In Islam:
- Quran 4:1, Hadith Bukhari 4:547-548
- Quran 7:189
- Hadith Bukhari 4:548
- Hadith Bukhari 4:547

In Christianity:
- Genesis 1:26-28
- Genesis 2:18
- Genesis 2:21-22
- Genesis 3

Evil

In Islam:
- Quran 3:54
- Quran 4:143, 17:16
- Quran 10:100
- Quran 17:16, 21

In Christianity:
- Numbers 23:19
- James 1:13
- John 3:16, Romans 5:8
- I John 1:5

Fasting – When and How

In Islam:
- Quran 2:185
- Hadith Bukhari 3:175
- Quran 2:187
- Also Quran 2:187

In Christianity:
- Matthew 6:16-18
- Psalm 69:10, Acts 14:23, Daniel 10, Matthew 4, Luke 2
- Matthew 4:2
- Daniel 10:2-3

Fasting – Why

In Islam:
- Quran 2:183
- Quran 2:185
- Quran 2:183
- Quran 33:35, 4:146

In Christianity:
- Psalm 35:13
- Luke 2:37
- Matthew 6:16-18
- Acts 4:12, John 14:6

Fate

In Islam:
- Quran 57:22
- Quran 6:125
- Quran 18:23-24
- Quran 6:48-49

In Christianity:
- James 5:16
- Psalm 49:13
- Proverbs 6:32
- Deuteronomy 30:19, Romans 6:6-7

Father/Master

In Islam:
- Hadith Bukhari 8:419
- Quran 19:93
- Quran 4:48
- Quran 112:3

In Christianity:
- Matthew 5:48, 6:9
- Deuteronomy 32:6
- Lamentations 2:11, Luke 13:34
- Romans 8:15

Founders

In Islam:
- Clinton Bennett, *In Search of Muhammad*. (New York: Continuum International Publishing Group, 1998), pp. 18–19
- Hadith Bukhari Book 1
- Quran 4:13-14, 3:32, 64:12, 5:92
- Quran 33:21, 24:54

In Christianity:
- Genesis 3:15, Isaiah 53, Matthew, Mark, Luke, and John
- Luke 1:3
- John 14:6
- John 10:30

Giving

In Islam:
- Quran 2:43
- Quran 5:12, 9:103
- Hadith Bukhari 2:534
- Hadith Muslim 51, Hadith Bukhari 2:585

In Christianity:
- Leviticus 27:30-32
- Proverbs 3:9-10
- 2 Corinthians 9:7
- Matthew 6:4

God

In Islam:
- Quran 1:1-2
- Quran 112:1-3
- Quran 2:106
- Quran 39:52, 2:186

In Christianity:
- Exodus 3:14
- John 3:16
- Psalm 119: 89, Malachi 3:6, John 1:1-3
- Romans 8:15, 23

The Gospel

In Islam:
- Quran 5:46
- Quran 7:157
- Quran 2:75, 3:78
- www.answering-islam.org/ Quran/Contra/injil_israel.html

In Christianity:
- I Timothy 3:16
- Galatians 1:11
- Luke 24:44
- Luke 1:1-4, I Corinthians 15:1

Hadith

In Islam:
- answering-islam.org/Index/H/ hadith.html
- answering-islam.org/Index/H/ hadith.html
- Quran 7:158
- www.answering-islam.org/Silas/ indexintro.htm

In Christianity:
- Mark 7:13
- I Corinthians 2:14
- John 14:25-27
- I Timothy 1:15, I Corinthians 12:13

Halal and Haram

In Islam:
- Quran 5:1
- Quran 5:3
- Quran 2:173
- Quran 3:104

In Christianity:
- I Corinthians 8:13
- Leviticus 11, Deuteronomy 14
- I Timothy 4:4
- Mark 2:13-17

Heaven

In Islam:
- Quran 78:31-36
- Quran 52:19-20
- Hadith Bukhari 6:402
- Quran 75:21-23, Hadith Bukhari 1:770

In Christianity:
- John 14:2
- Philippians 3:20-21
- Matthew 22:30
- Revelation 4

Hell

In Islam:
- Quran 33:64
- Quran 35:36-37
- Quran 19:71
- Hadith Muslim 1139

In Christianity:
- 2 Thessalonians 1:8-9
- Matthew 13:42
- Hebrews 10:26-27
- Philippians 1:22-24, 2 Corinthians 5:8

Jerusalem

In Islam:
- Quran 17:1
- Quran 17:1
- Hadith Bukhari 4:429, 5:227
- Quran 17:1

In Christianity:
- www.theopedia.com/Proof_ texting
- Luke 19:28-47
- Joshua 15:63, Judges 1:21, 2 Samuel 5:6-10, 7:1, Deuteronomy 12:10
- Zechariah 12:1-13

Jesus

In Islam:
- Quran 43:59
- Quran 9:30
- Quran 3:49
- Quran 4:157

In Christianity:
- John 1:1
- Matthew 16:16, Matthew 4:1-11
- Matthew 8:16, John 11:1-44.
- Matthew 27:27-56, Mark 15:21-38, Luke 23:26-49, John 19:16-37

Jihad – Holy War

In Islam:
- Quran 2:216
- Quran 47:4
- Quran 8:39
- www.answering-islam.org/ Gilchrist/Vol1/4b.html

In Christianity:
- Romans 13:1-7
- Deuteronomy 12:29-31
- I Chronicles 22:7-10
- Luke 6:27-28

Jihad – Inner Strife:

In Islam:
- Quran 22:78
- Quran 29:6
- Quran 25:52
- Quran 49:15

In Christianity:
- John 3:30
- Romans 12:1-2
- James 1:2-4
- Galatians 5:24-25

Language

In Islam:
- Quran 12:2
- Quran 20:113
- Quran 44:58
- Hadith Ibn Majah: Zuhd 32, Hadith Ahmad Ibn Hanbal: Musnad 3, 40

In Christianity:
- Acts 2:8-11
- Mark 16:15-16
- Matthew 24:14
- Revelation 5:9

Lying

In Islam:
- Quran 2:225
- Quran 5:89
- Quran 16:106
- Hadith Bukhari 3:857

In Christianity:
- Matthew 5:37
- Revelation 22:15
- Matthew 12:31
- John 8:44

Marriage – Framework

In Islam:
- Quran 4:3
- Hadith Abu Dawud 848, 849
- Quran 4:4
- Hadith Bukhari 7:4

In Christianity:
- Genesis 2:24
- Malachi 2:14
- Ephesians 5:25
- Hebrews 13:4, I Corinthians 7:7-8

Marriage – Polygamy

In Islam:
- Quran 4:3
- Quran 4:24
- Quran 4:24, 24:33
- Quran 33:50

In Christianity:
- Mark 10:6-9
- Genesis 4
- Matthew 19:6
- Numbers 20:12,
  1 Samuel 2:12-36

Marriage Relationship

In Islam:
- Hadith Bukhari 1:301
- Quran 3:14
- Quran 2:223
- Quran 4:34

In Christianity:
- Ephesians 5:25
- Ephesians 5:28
- Colossians 3:19
- 1 Peter 3:7

Martyrdom

In Islam:
- Quran 2:216, 61:11, 2:244
- Quran 9:111
- Quran 4:74
- Quran 4:69-73

In Christianity:
- 1 John 3:16
- 2 Corinthians 12:10, Acts
  chapters 6 and 7
- Romans 6:23
- Ephesians 2:8-9

Miracles

In Islam:
- Quran 6:109, 29:50
- Quran 17:101, 3:49
- Quran 10:20
- Quran 26:190-195

In Christianity:
- 1 Kings 18
- Exodus 5, Psalm 77:11-14
- John 5:36
- Matthew 4:23, 14:15-21,
  Luke 7:12-16

Original Sin

In Islam:
- Quran17:15
- Quran 2:37, 39:53, 35:18
- Hadith Bukhari 4:506
- Quran 17:21, 2:177

In Christianity:
- Romans 5:12
- Romans 3:23, Psalm 51:5
- 1 Peter 5:8, 2 Corinthians 11:3
- Romans 6:23

Pilgrimage

In Islam:
- Quran 3:97,
  Hadith Bukhari 2:596
- Quran 2:196
- Quran 2:197
- Quran 2:198-201

In Christianity:
- Hebrews 11:13
- Examples of places Jesus visited:
  Mark 11:1-11
- John 4:21-23
- Psalm 119:54, Hebrews 11:12-14

Prayer – How Often

In Islam:
- Hadith Bukhari 1:63
- Hadith Bukhari 1:345
- Quran 17:78-79,
  Hadith Bukhari 1:500
- Hadith al-Tirmidhi 379

In Christianity:
- Luke 18:1, Ephesians 6:18
- Luke 11:1-4
- Matthew 6:9-13
- 1 Thessalonians 5:16-18

Prayer – Method

In Islam:
- Quran 5:6
- Quran 4:43
- Quran. 4:102
- Quran 12:2

In Christianity:
- Nehemiah 2:4-5,
  Ephesians 6:18
- James 4:8
- Romans 8:26-27
- 1 Kings 8:54, Exodus 4:31,
  2 Chronicles 20:18;
  Matthew 26:39, 1 Kings 8:22

Prayer – Purpose

In Islam:
- Quran 2:238
- Quran 29:45
- Quran 35:29-30
- Quran 11:114

In Christianity:
- Philippians 4:6-7
- Psalm 148, 150
- 1 Peter 5:7, 1 Timothy 2:1-3
- Psalm 37:7

Prophet

In Islam:
- Quran 2:213
- Quran 23:23
- Quran 2:136
- Quran 33:40

In Christianity:
- 1 Samuel 3, Exodus 3
- Deuteronomy 18:19-22
- Jeremiah 28:9
- 1 John 4:1-3

Salvation

In Islam:
- Quran 39:74
- Quran 18:107, 2:81
- Quran 21:47
- Quran 19:71

In Christianity:
- Romans 10:9-13
- John 14:6
- James 2:18
- John 3:16

Satan

In Islam:
- Quran 38:76, 15:27
- Quran 17:61, 18:50
- Quran 38:76
- Hadith Bukhari 4:641

In Christianity:
- Ezekiel 28:13-19
- 1 Peter 5:8, Luke10:17-19
- Isaiah 14:12-17
- Luke 4:1-7, John 12:31

Second Coming

In Islam:
- Quran 43:61
- Hadith Bukhari 3:425
- Quran 4:159
- Hadith Abu-Dawood - 2025

In Christianity:
- 1 Timothy 4:1, John 5:22
- Philippians 2:10
- 2 Corinthians 5:10, Matthew 19:28-30
- Isaiah 9:7, Acts 1:11

Sharia Law

In Islam:
- www.light-of-life.com/eng/answer/a4990efm.htm
- Quran 6:153, 33:36
- Quran 5:101
- Quran 24:2

In Christianity:
- Romans 2:14-16
- Romans 7:12
- 1 John 5:3
- Luke 20:25

Sin

In Islam:
- Quran 25:70
- Quran 91:7-8
- Quran 7:178
- Quran 24:33, 4:24, 2:225

In Christianity:
- Hebrews 3:8, Genesis 4:6-7
- James 1:13
- Joshua 24:15, Deuteronomy 30:19
- James 2:10

Slave or Child

In Islam:
- Quran 39:10
- Quran 2:195
- Quran 19:96
- Quran 3:32, 9:5, 9:29

In Christianity:
- 1 John 3:1
- 1 John 4:10
- Matthew 5:45
- Titus 3:5

Son of God

In Islam:
- Quran 19:35, 23:91
- Quran 4:171, 37:152
- Quran 10:68, 6:101
- Quran 9:30

In Christianity:
- Isaiah 9:6-7
- Luke 1:34
- John 1:1
- Matthew 3:17, 17:5

Sons of Abraham

In Islam:
- Quran 37:99-106
- Quran 37:107
- Quran. 2:127
- Quran 14:39

In Christianity:
- Genesis 22:2
- Genesis 17:20-21
- Genesis 21:20-21, 25:12-18
- Hebrews 11:17

Spiritual Beings

In Islam:
- Quran 72:1-2, 34:12
- Quran 15:27
- Hadith Muslim 1399
- Quran 66:6

In Christianity:
- Galatians 3:19
- Psalm 34:7
- Revelations 7:11
- Revelations 12:7-9

The Ten Commandments

In Islam:
- Quran 7:145
- Quran 7:150-154
- Quran 6:151-153, 17:23-29
- Quran 17:23-29

In Christianity:
- Exodus 20
- Exodus 32:19
- Exodus 34:1
- Luke 10:25-37, Romans 2:13, Galatians 3:24

Trinity

In Islam:
- Quran 112:1
- Quran 4:171
- Quran 5:116
- Quran 5:73

In Christianity:
- Deuteronomy 6:4
- Galatians 4:4-6
- Matthew 3:16-17
- John1:1, Mark 9:7

The Veil

In Islam:
- Hadith Bukhari 1:148
- Quran 24:31
- Quran 33:59
- Quran 33:32-33

In Christianity:
- 1 Timothy 2:9
- Genesis 1:27
- 2 Corinthians 3:16-17
- James 1:21-25

Women – Equality

In Islam:
- Quran 4:34
- Quran 2:228, Hadith Bukhari 1:28, 4:548
- Hadith Bukhari 1:301
- Hadith Abu-Dawood: 2078, 2080

In Christianity:
- Genesis 1:27
- Galatians 3:26-29
- Acts 9:36-38
- Acts 1:8

Women – Salvation

In Islam:
- Hadith Bukhari 1:28
- Quran 33:33
- Hadith Bukhari 7:121
- Quran 38:52, 56:17

In Christianity:
- John 6:40
- Galatians 3:26-29
- Ephesians 5:22
- Romans 10:13

Women – Witness

In Islam:
- Quran 2:282
- Hadith Bukhari 3:826
- Quran 4:11
- Quran 4:548

In Christianity:
- Mark 16:9-10
- Matthew 12:49-50
- Psalm 103:13
- Philippians 4:3, Romans 8:17

Works

In Islam:
- Quran 99:6-8
- Quran 2:177
- Quran 5:55
- Quran 2:195

In Christianity:
- James 2:26
- Mark 12:31
- Roman 10:9, Ephesians 2:8-9
- Romans 5:1

The Written Revelation

In Islam:
- Quran 48:29
- www.answering-islam.org/Quran/
- Quran 56:77-79
- www.answering-islam.org/Quran/

In Christianity:
- 2 Timothy 3:16
- www.truthnet.org/Bible-Origins/
- www.answersingenesis.org/articles/am/v6/n2/unity-bible
- Hebrews 4:12, Psalm 33:11, 93:5, 119:89

QUESTIONS?

If you have questions about what you have read, or if you want to pray with someone, we encourage you to contact us:

Call of Love Ministries
Tel: 832-220-4040
Email: info@calloflove.org
P.O. Box 498698
Cincinnati, OH 45249 USA